THE PURITANS
DAY BY DAY

Because you are but a young man, beware of temptations and snares; and above all, be careful to keep yourself in the use of means; resort to good company; and howbeit you be nicknamed a Puritan, and mocked, yet care not for that, but rejoice and be glad, that they who are scorned and scoffed by this godless and vain world, and nicknamed Puritans, would admit you to their society; for I must tell you, when I am at this point as you see me, I get no comfort to my soul by any second means under heaven but from those who are nicknamed Puritans. They are the men that can give a word of comfort to a wearied soul in due season, and that I have found by experience ....

THE LAST AND HEAVENLY SPEECHES, AND GLORIOUS DEPARTURE,
OF JOHN, VISCOUNT KENMURE.

SOME RELATED TITLES FROM THE BANNER OF TRUTH TRUST

Voices from the Past, Puritan Devotional Readings, vols. 1 & 2, ed. Richard Rushing

Jewels from John Newton, ed. Miller Ferrie

The Loveliness of Christ, Samuel Rutherford

None But Jesus, John Flavel

Smooth Stones Taken from Ancient Brooks, C. H. Spurgeon

Daily Prayer and Praise, vols 1 & 2

Words Old and New, Horatius Bonar

Expository Thoughts on the Gospels, 7 vols, J. C. Ryle

The Golden Treasury of Puritan Quotations, I. D. E. Thomas

The Valley of Vision (Print and Audio CD versions)

Treasury of His Promises, J. Graham Miller

Susannah Spurgeon: Free Grace and Dying Love

A Way to Pray, Matthew Henry

A Guide to Prayer, Isaac Watts

Grace in Winter: Rutherford in Verse, Faith Cook

Calvin's Wisdom: An Anthology, J. Graham Miller

The Banner of Truth Trust originated in 1957 in London. The founders believed that much of the best literature of historic Christianity had been allowed to fall into oblivion and that, under God, its recovery could well lead not only to a strengthening of the church, but to true revival.

Inter-denominational in vision, this publishing work is now international, and our lists include a number of contemporary authors as well as classics from the past. The translation of these books into many languages is encouraged.

A monthly magazine, *The Banner of Truth,* is also published. More information about this and all our publications can be found on our website or supplied by either of the offices below.

THE BANNER OF TRUTH TRUST

3 Murrayfield Road
Edinburgh, EH12 6EL
UK

PO Box 621, Carlisle
Pennsylvania 17013,
USA

www.banneroftruth.org

THE PURITANS
DAY BY DAY

Compiled by

H. J. HORN

THE BANNER OF TRUTH TRUST

THE BANNER OF TRUTH TRUST
3 Murrayfield Road, Edinburgh EH12 6EL, UK
P.O. Box 621, Carlisle, PA 17013, USA

✤

© The Banner of Truth Trust 2016
First published in 1928 as *The Puritan Remembrancer*
by Stanley Martin & Co. Ltd., London

✤

ISBN:
Print: 978 1 84871 707 7
EPUB: 978 1 84871 708 4
Kindle: 978 1 84871 709 1

✤

Typeset in 10.5 /13.5 pt Adobe Garamond Pro
at the Banner of Truth Trust, Edinburgh

Printed in the USA by
Versa Press, Inc.,
East Peoria, IL

✤

FOREWORD

EVERYONE knows the value and the power of a brief clear-edged and arresting saying. It is a light that illumines a dark bit of a man's mind. It is a seed which generates, often unconsciously, to appear in some living truth, in after days. It is a cup of cold water to a thirsty soul. It is sometimes a voice that seems to call with a human tone from far up on the heights. A reader has the common experience of following many of the sentences on the page of his book only to find himself unlessoned and untouched in interest until he begins to be weary, when some short, crisp, unexpected saying holds him, and he finds it to be treasure hid in the field.

Here in this unique selection from a wide range of reading we have a noble army of memorable aphorisms. They have been found chiefly in the writings of the Puritan worthies, who excelled in their power of deep insight, both in the word of God and the heart of man, with the rare gift of quaint and distinctive expression. However, Mr Horn has not confined himself to these, but has travelled in a wide round of devotional literature, and many of the sayings are as fresh and new as they are piquant and tender.

Young preachers should keep this volume, with its careful ordering, and its full indexes, lying at their right hand, and in days when the mind is dull and the spirit is weary, they will find it to be the brook in the way.

W. M. CLOW.

PREFACE

IT is written of King Solomon that 'he spake three thousand proverbs'. Merely to compile and arrange the three thousand sayings in this little book has occupied odd moments during five and twenty years!

To acknowledge indebtedness in a book of this kind is unnecessary, but it is only honest to say, that while the greater part of these pithy sentences has been found in the course of my own reading of the authors' works, I am indebted for additions to my store to Spurgeon's *Treasury of David*, and to Dr Moffatt's *Golden Book of John Owen*.

As would only have been expected some authors have yielded far more freely than others. One could not read much in John Trapp's quaint commentary, or in Henry Smith's pair of volumes, or Secker's alliterative pages, without finding gems of expression. On the other hand Thomas Goodwin's style does not lend itself to aphorisms and one may read many of his pages without finding a single quaint remark. It must be understood, that, while the greater part of the book is Puritan, the word is used rather for the period than of the persons quoted. Desiring variety, as well as truth, I have sought among many authors and there are quotations here from over a hundred writers, though some of them are represented by only a few sentences.

I am deeply indebted to Principal W. M. Clow, D.D., for suggesting the title,* for most kind and helpful advice as to

---

* Originally published as *The Puritan Remembrancer*.

arrangement of matter, as well as for encouragement to publish and for generously writing a Foreword.

Some of my brethren in the ministry may find a suggestion or two of homiletic value in the texts and headings, and it may be that some reader may be induced to study for himself the writings of the Puritans from whose glowing forges many of these flying sparks have come.

H. J. HORN
Purley, Surrey
October, 1928

PROVERBS are the extracts of experience wrought out by practice.—THOMAS ADAMS.

❧

BECAUSE the preacher was wise ... he pondered, and sought out, and set in order many proverbs.—ECCLES. 12:9. (R.V.)

❧

THE first and second King of Peace taught much by parables and proverbs.—THOMAS ADAMS.

❧

1 January

CHRIST PRE-EMINENT

That in all things he might have the pre-eminence.—Col. 1:18.

WE must not heed what others did who were before us, but what Christ did who was before all.—THOMAS FULLER.

If Christ stand with us who can withstand us?—JOHN BOYS.

When the sun is up, the moon seemeth to have no light.
—GEORGE ESTEY.

Christ is figured in the law, foretold in the prophets, and fulfilled in the gospel.—HENRY SMITH.

The 'Ancient of Days' is to be served before all that are younger than himself.—STEPHEN CHARNOCK.

We may hear the gospel of life, but not the life of the gospel, without him.—THOMAS FULLER.

Christ is the native subject on which all preaching should run.—JAMES DURHAM.

Christ is the scope of the Scripture.—RICHARD SIBBES.

2 JANUARY

SILENCE

Even a fool, when he holdeth his peace, is counted wise: and he that shutteth his lips is esteemed a man of understanding.—Prov. 17:28.

SILENCE is so rare a virtue where wisdom regulates it, that it is accounted a virtue where folly imposes it.—THOMAS BROOKS.

A fool is hardly discerned when silent; his picture is best taken when he is speaking.—WILLIAM JENKYN.

Some, like Balaam's ass, scarce ever open their mouths twice.
—THOMAS ADAMS.

A man may wrong another as well by silence as by slander.
—THOMAS WATSON.

Speech is then only good when it is better than silence.
—RICHARD SIBBES.

As he cannot be wise who speaks much, so he cannot be known for a fool that says nothing.—THOMAS BROOKS.

Either keep silence, or speak that which is better than silence.
—JOHN TRAPP.

Silence is the daughter of shamefacedness.—THOMAS ADAMS.

3 JANUARY

PERSONAL ACCOUNTABILITY

But every one shall die for his own iniquity.—Jer. 31:30.
The son shall not bear the iniquity of the father, neither shall the father bear the iniquity of the son.—Ezek. 18:20.

IF thy father be holy for himself, and thee too, he shall go to heaven for himself, and thee too.—WILLIAM JENKYN.

One bird cannot fly to heaven with another bird's wings.
—THOMAS ADAMS.

He that goeth to church by an attorney, shall go to heaven also by a proxy.—JOHN BOYS.

The fire is our wood, though it be the devil's flame.
—THOMAS BROOKS.

The devil's faith cannot save us, no more than it can save him.
—HENRY SMITH.

Is not he as much guilty of his own death that rejects a medicine, as he that cuts his own throat?—STEPHEN CHARNOCK.

In Gideon's camp every soldier had his own pitcher.
—THOMAS ADAMS.

4 JANUARY

ESAU'S REPENTANCE

When he [Esau] afterward desired to inherit the blessing, he was rejected (for he found no place of repentance), though he sought it diligently with tears.—Heb. 12:17. (R.V.)

HIS is like weeping with an onion; the eye sheds tears because it smarts.—WILLIAM SECKER.

The eye may be watery and the heart flinty. An apricot may be soft without, but it has a hard stone within.
—THOMAS WATSON.

Sin may be the occasion of great sorrow when there is no sorrow for sin.—JOHN OWEN.

Esau cried, not for his sin in selling the birthright, but for his loss in missing the blessing.—JOHN TRAPP.

Some tears God hath no bottle for.—RICHARD SIBBES.

Many have the space of repentance who have not the grace of repentance.—WILLIAM SECKER.

Esau wept that he lost the blessing, not that he sold it.
—WILLIAM GURNALL.

5 JANUARY

MERCIES

I am returned to Jerusalem with mercies.—Zech. 1:16.

MERCIES are such gifts as advance our debts.
—WILLIAM SECKER.

Mercies are never so savoury as when they savour of a Saviour.
—RALPH VENNING.

Wicked men have mercies by providence, not by virtue of a covenant; with God's leave, not with his love.
—THOMAS WATSON.

Christians have two sorts of goods: the goods of the throne and the goods of the footstool; moveables and immoveables.
—JOHN FLAVEL.

Outward things are the gifts of God, and he doth not value them at so high a rate as we do. He doth not care if his enemies have them.—EDWARD MARBURY.

Every true son of Jacob will be content to part with his broth for the birthright.—JOHN TRAPP.

God doth not parcel himself out by retail, but gives his saints leave to challenge whatever he hath as theirs.
—WILLIAM GURNALL.

6 January

GOD'S STRANGE INSTRUMENTS

I girded thee, though thou hast not known me.—Isa. 45:5.
*The men ... [heathens] said unto him,
[Jonah] Why hast thou done this?*—Jon. 1:10.

GOD can make a straight stroke with a crooked stick.
—THOMAS WATSON.

Though it be clay, let Christ use it, and it shall open the eyes, though in itself more like to put them out.
—WILLIAM GURNALL.

The most crooked tree will make timber for the temple, if God please to hew it.—THOMAS FULLER.

A man may be a false prophet and yet speak the truth.
—RICHARD SIBBES.

Peter hath a cock to tell him cowardice, and Balaam an ass to reprove his avarice.
—THOMAS ADAMS.

The Assyrian did a divine work against Jerusalem, but not with a divine end.—STEPHEN CHARNOCK.

I have seen a dull whetstone set an edge on a knife.
—THOMAS FULLER.

7 JANUARY

ETERNITY

Eternity.—Isa. 57:15.
Eternal.—2 Cor. 4:18.

WHATSOEVER is eternal is immutable.
—STEPHEN CHARNOCK.

If you look past the world, you put your head up into eternity.
—THOMAS GOODWIN.

As nothing eternal is created, so nothing created is eternal.
—STEPHEN CHARNOCK.

This infinite cipher, *ever*, which, though it stand for nothing in the vulgar account, yet contains all our millions.
—GEORGE SWINNOCK.

Mutability and eternity are utterly inconsistent.
—STEPHEN CHARNOCK.

Eternity is an everlasting *Now.*—CHRISTOPHER NESSE.

Eternity is the duration of God's essence.
—STEPHEN CHARNOCK.

There is no wrinkle on the brow of eternity.
—THOMAS MANTON.

8 January

PERSECUTION

Yea, and all that will live godly in Christ Jesus shall suffer persecution.
—2 Tim. 3:12.

PERSECUTION is the black angel that dodges the church, the red horse that follows the white at the heels.
—JOHN TRAPP.

True godliness is that which breeds the quarrel between God's children and the wicked.—JOHN DOD.

Christians must be thrown to the lions because they are Christians.—NEHEMIAH ROGERS.

Cold blasts make a fire to flame the higher and burn the better.—GEORGE SWINNOCK.

Gold may be gold, and bear the king's stamp upon it, when it is trampled upon by men.—SAMUEL RUTHERFORD.

Saints must be best in worst times.—JOHN TRAPP.

Our help is in the name of the Lord, but our fears are in the name of man.—WILLIAM GREENHILL.

9 January

THE WILL FOR THE DEED

Thou didst well that it was in thine heart.—1 Kings 8:18.
The desire of a man is the measure of his kindness.—Prov. 19:22. (R.V.)
If the readiness is there, it is acceptable.—2 Cor. 8:12. (R.V.)

GOD accepts the will for the deed, only where the impediments and hindrances are impossible to be removed.
—RICHARD SIBBES.

God looks more at our wills than at our works.
—WILLIAM SECKER.

God does sometimes accept of willingness without the work, but never the work without the willingness.
—THOMAS WATSON.

Good intentions do no more make a good action than a fair mark makes a good shot.—WILLIAM GURNALL.

Purpose without performance is like a cloud without rain.
—NEHEMIAH ROGERS.

A heart without a gift is better than a gift without a heart.
—WILLIAM SECKER.

What the foot is to the body the will is to the soul.
—WILLIAM GURNALL.

10 January

THE CROSS

The cross of our Lord Jesus Christ.—Gal. 6:14.

THE cross was the first general rendezvous in this world.
—THOMAS GOODWIN.

There is no tribunal so magnificent, no throne so stately, no show of triumph so distinguished, no chariot so elevated, as is the gibbet on which Christ hath subdued death and the devil.—JOHN CALVIN.

The church is heir to the cross.—THOMAS ADAMS.

He suffered not *as* God, but he suffered who *was* God.
—JOHN OWEN.

Christ was offered twice; first in the temple, which is called his morning sacrifice; then on the cross, which is termed his evening sacrifice. In the one he was redeemed, in the other he did redeem.—JOHN BOYS.

The doctrine of the death of Christ is the substance of the gospel.—STEPHEN CHARNOCK.

11 January

KNOWLEDGE

The heart of him that hath understanding seeketh knowledge.
—Prov. 15:14.

JULIANUS, the lawyer, said that when he had one foot in the grave, yet he would have the other in the school.
—JOHN TRAPP.

Opinion in good men is but knowledge in the making.
—JOHN MILTON.

True knowledge and profession of knowledge are distinct.
—STEPHEN CHARNOCK.

True faith and saving knowledge go together.
—GEORGE SWINNOCK.

Knowledge carries the torch before faith.—THOMAS WATSON.

Knowledge directs conscience, conscience perfects knowledge.—THOMAS ADAMS.

Knowledge and love, like the water and the ice, beget each other.—THOMAS BROOKS.

Knowledge in the head is as money in the purse, knowledge in the heart is as money for our use.—STEPHEN CHARNOCK.

12 January

MARTYRS

I saw under the altar the souls of them that were slain for the word of God, and for the testimony which they held.—Rev. 6:9.

MARTYRS are the eldest sons of blessedness among all the sons of adoption.—THOMAS GOODWIN.

Martyrdom came into the world early; the first man that died, died for religion.—WILLIAM JENKYN.

Two things especially commend a martyr: faith in Christ, and love to the church.—JOHN BOYS.

The bloodiest tragedies in the world have been acted upon the stage of the church.—WILLIAM GURNALL.

Abel was the first martyr in God's calendar.

—THOMAS GOODWIN.

The best of saints have borne the worst of sufferings.

—GEORGE SWINNOCK.

The martyrs shook the powers of darkness with the irresistible power of weakness.—JOHN MILTON.

13 January

TRUTH AND ERROR

The spirit of truth, and the spirit of error.—1 John 4:6.

TRUTH with self-denial, a better pennyworth than error with all its flesh-pleasing.—WILLIAM GURNALL.

Every truth, like a lease, brings in revenue the next year as well as this.—WILLIAM JENKYN.

Better to present truth in her native plainness than to hang her ears with counterfeit pearls.—THOMAS BROOKS.

What usage truth finds, that her followers must expect.
—WILLIAM GURNALL.

There is but one truth, yet errors about truth are divers.
—THOMAS GOODWIN.

One error is a bridge to another.—WILLIAM JENKYN.

Love is the best entertainer of truth.—RICHARD SIBBES.

News may come that truth is sick, but never that it is dead.
—WILLIAM GURNALL.

14 JANUARY

ZEAL

He [Phineas] was zealous for my sake.—Num. 25:11.

ZEAL is the heat or intension* of the affections.
—GEORGE SWINNOCK.

One live coal may set a whole stack on fire.—JOHN TRAPP.

Zeal is like resin to the bow-strings, without which the lute makes no music.—THOMAS WATSON.

Zeal (as one saith) is the dagger which love draws in God's quarrel.—JOHN FLAVEL.

Discretion without zeal is slow-paced, and zeal without discretion is heady; let, therefore, zeal spur on discretion, and discretion rein in zeal.—GEORGE SWINNOCK.

However zeal may be censured for frenzy, it's but the same livery that Festus bestowed on Paul.—HENRY WILKINSON.

Zeal is like fire; in the chimney it is one of the best servants, but out of the chimney it is one of the worst masters.
—THOMAS BROOKS.

---

* Intensity or intensification.

15 January

SUICIDE

Saul took a sword, and fell upon it.—1 Sam. 31:4.
Ahithophel ... hanged himself, and died.—2 Sam. 17:23.

NO creature but man willingly kills itself.
—THOMAS WATSON.

We may not ourselves loose our souls, but let God let them out of prison.—JOHN BOYS.

No man must let the tenant out of the tenement till God the landlord call for it.—THOMAS ADAMS.

Man was not born of his own pleasure, neither must he die at his own lust.—HENRY SMITH.

Judas hanged himself to quiet his conscience.
—THOMAS WATSON.

He that would not die when he must, and he that would die when he must not, are both of them cowards alike.
—GEORGE SWINNOCK.

As we cannot live without a *permittis*, so we must not die without a *dimittis*.*—THOMAS ADAMS.

---

* Permittis = a permit; dimittis = a release.

16 January

MERCIES FORFEITED

How many hired servants of my father's have bread enough and to spare, and I perish with hunger!—Luke 15:17.

THE best way for Christians not to be losers of what they have, is to be labourers for what they want.

—WILLIAM JENKYN.

It is just with God to make men want that to supply their necessity which they have mis-spended upon their nicety.

—THOMAS FULLER.

God loves to let us see the worth of his favours by the want of them.—JOHN TRAPP.

It is just with God that they should feel the curse of anarchy who never were thankful for regular dominion.

—WILLIAM JENKYN.

We forfeit many favours by over-affecting them.—JOHN TRAPP.

Mercies are best known by the lack, and most prized when most wanted.—JOHN FLAVEL.

How good is God to deny us mercies in mercy.

—WILLIAM JENKYN.

17 JANUARY

ASSURANCE AND FAITH

Draw near with a true heart in full assurance of faith.—Heb. 10:22.
Faith is the assurance of things hoped for.—Heb. 11:1. (R.V.)

ASSURANCE is a fruit that grows out of the root of faith.
—STEPHEN CHARNOCK.

Faith cannot be lost, but assurance may; therefore assurance is not faith.—THOMAS BROOKS.

Assurance is, as it were, the cream of faith.—WILLIAM GURNALL.

Faith is our seal; assurance of faith is God's seal.
—CHRISTOPHER NESSE.

Reason's arm is too short to reach the jewel of assurance.
—THOMAS BROOKS.

Assurance saith, I believe my sins are pardoned through Christ; faith's language is, I believe on Christ for the pardon of them.—WILLIAM GURNALL.

Sin can never quite bereave a saint of his jewel, his grace; but it may steal away the key of the cabinet, his assurance.
—WILLIAM JENKYN.

18 JANUARY

SIN—ITS OWN PUNISHMENT

Sin, when it is fullgrown, bringeth forth death.—James 1:15. (R.V.)

SIN is the weight on the clock which makes the hammer to strike.—GEORGE SWINNOCK.

He that travails with mischief conceives sorrow.
—JOHN BUNYAN.

If there were no justice to revenge sin, sin would be vengeance to itself.—ELISHA COLES.

You began to be mortal when you began to be sinful.
—WILLIAM SECKER.

Sin is the greatest punishment of sin.—JOHN BOYS.

All misery calleth sin mother.—GEORGE SWINNOCK.

Sin carrieth two rods about it, shame and fear.
—EDWARD MARBURY.

Sin and shame came in both together.—CHRISTOPHER NESSE.

Death waits upon sin as the wages on the work.
—THOMAS TAYLOR.

19 January

THANKFULNESS

Be ye thankful.—Col. 3:15.
In every thing give thanks.—1 Thess. 5:18.
Giving thanks always for all things.—Eph. 5:20.

AS the Lord loveth a cheerful giver, so likewise a cheerful thanksgiver.—JOHN BOYS.

Faith that receiveth grace returneth glory.—THOMAS MANTON.

The life of thankfulness consisteth in the thankfulness of thy life.—GEORGE SWINNOCK.

Thanks must be given and held as still due.—JOHN TRAPP.

He enjoys much who is thankful for a little.—WILLIAM SECKER.

The thankfulness of the receiver ought to answer unto the benefit of the bestower, as the echo answereth to the voice.—THOMAS FULLER.

It is very gross to thank God only in gross, and not in parcel.
—JOHN BOYS.

20 JANUARY

THE BENEFIT OF AFFLICTION

It is good for me that I have been afflicted.—Psa. 119:71.
Jonah prayed unto the Lord his God out of the fish's belly.—Jon. 2:1.

AFFLICTION is God's flail to thresh off our husks.
—THOMAS WATSON.

As Jacob was blessed and halted both at one time, so a man may be blessed and afflicted both together.—HENRY SMITH.

Troubles are free schoolmasters.—JOHN TRAPP.

The whale which swallowed Jonah was the means of bringing him safe to land.—THOMAS WATSON.

As the hotter the day, the greater the dew at night; so the hotter the time of trouble, the greater the dews of refreshing from God.—JOHN TRAPP.

Jonah was sent into the whale's belly to make his sermon for Nineveh.—THOMAS WATSON.

God uses the captivity of the people to enlarge the bounds of the gospel.—STEPHEN CHARNOCK.

21 January

HYPOCRITES AND HEAVEN

He [Balaam] took up his parable, and said… Let me die the death of the righteous, and let my last end be like his!—Num. 23:7, 10.

BALAAM himself likes one end of the piece; he would die like a righteous man, though live like a wizard as he was.
—WILLIAM GURNALL.

We must not think to dance with the devil all day and sup with Christ at night.—JOHN TRAPP.

They are unbelievers who, though they would have the safety Christ has purchased, will not pay him the services he hath merited.—STEPHEN CHARNOCK.

The hypocrite desires holiness only as a bridge to heaven.
—JOSEPH ALLEINE.

An hypocrite cometh hardlier to heaven than a gross sinner, and hath far more obstacles.—JOHN TRAPP.

The old heart cannot sing the new song.—CHRISTOPHER NESSE.

22 JANUARY

AFFECTIONS

Set your affection on things above.—Col. 3:2.
Your own affections.—2 Cor. 6:12. (R.V.)

THE affections are as the master-workmen which set our thoughts on work.—WILLIAM GURNALL.

A man without affections is like the Dead Sea that moves not at all.—RICHARD SIBBES.

Christianity doth not abrogate affections, but regulates them.
—THOMAS MANTON.

A man must first love that he would be, before he can be that which he loveth.—ANDREW WILLETT.

Grace comes not to take away a man's affections, but to take them up.—WILLIAM FENNER.

Isaac was not more blind in his eyes than in his affection to his first-born.—JOHN TRAPP.

Affections should be the spiritual wings of the soul.
—RICHARD SIBBES.

Much action and little affection avails not.
—CHRISTOPHER NESSE.

23 JANUARY

EXPERIENCE

I have learned by experience.—Gen. 30:27.
Consider from this day and upward ... through all that time.
—Hag. 2:15, 16. (R.V.)
And experience, hope.—Rom. 5:4.

HE who hath found God present in one extremity may trust him in the next.—JOHN TRAPP.

Not to try before we trust, is want of wisdom; not to trust after we have tried, is want of charity.—THOMAS FULLER.

It is a ... spiritually wholesome and refreshful air that breathes in that walk betwixt Ebenezer and Jehovah-Jireh.
—JOSEPH CHURCH.

Why should we fear that arm of God should be too short for others, that could reach us?—THOMAS FULLER.

Experiences are like crutches, which do indeed make a lame man to go, but they do not make the lame man sound.
—WILLIAM GURNALL.

Bought wit is ever best prized.—JOHN TRAPP.

24 JANUARY

REPENTANCE

Repentance from dead works.—Heb. 6:1.
Repentance unto life.—Acts 11:18.
Repentance toward God.—Acts 20:21.

REPENTANCE, that fair and happy daughter of an ugly and odious mother.—JOHN TRAPP.

You cannot repent too soon, because you do not know how soon it may be too late.—THOMAS FULLER.

Godly sorrow will eat up worldly, as Moses' rod did the rods of the magicians.—GEORGE SWINNOCK.

Only the great heart-maker can be the great heart-breaker.
—RICHARD BAXTER.

It is our duty to feel sin, to fear sin, to fly sin as far as we can.
—JOHN BOYS.

Penitency and pain are words of one derivation, and very near of kin.—JOHN TRAPP.

Though repentance be the act of man, yet it is the gift of God.—WILLIAM SECKER.

25 JANUARY

YIELDING TO TEMPTATION

She pressed him [Samson] daily ... and urged him ... that he told her all his heart.—Judg. 16:16, 17.

THOU temptest God to suffer thy locks to be cut when thou art so bold as to lay thy head in the lap of a temptation.
—WILLIAM GURNALL.

It is not falling into the water, but lying in the water, that drowns.—THOMAS BROOKS.

The devil got in at first into men's heart by his ear.
—GEORGE SWINNOCK.

If you hold the stirrup, no wonder if Satan get into the saddle.—WILLIAM SECKER.

It is not the laying the bait hurts the fish, if the fish do not bite.
—THOMAS WATSON.

If we would not yield to the sin, sit not at the door of the occasion.
—WILLIAM GURNALL.

Man had a tempter and the devil had none.
—STEPHEN CHARNOCK.

26 JANUARY

WITNESS-BEARING

We cannot but speak the things which we have seen and heard.
—Acts 4:20.

A true witness delivereth souls.—Prov. 14:25.

HE is a base servant that is ashamed of his lord's livery.
—GEORGE SWINNOCK.

Among all God's children there is not one possessed with a dumb devil.—THOMAS BROOKS.

Love will stammer rather than be dumb.—ROBERT LEIGHTON.

Did Christ open his veins for our redemption, and shall not we open our mouths for his vindication?—WILLIAM SECKER.

The light of religion ought not to be carried in a dark lantern.
—GEORGE SWINNOCK.

If a man have faith within, it will break forth at the mouth.
—THOMAS HOOKER.

How shall those stand for Christ who never stood in Christ?
—WILLIAM SECKER.

27 JANUARY

AFFLICTION IN GLORY

For our light affliction, which is but for a moment, worketh for us a far more exceeding and eternal weight of glory.—2 Cor. 4:17.

Partakers of Christ's sufferings; that, when his glory shall be revealed, ye may be glad also.—1 Pet. 4:13.

DISGRACE may be the way to glory.—GEORGE SWINNOCK.

Losses and disgraces are the wheels of Christ's triumphant chariot.—SAMUEL RUTHERFORD.

Shall light troubles make you forget weighty mercies?
—JOHN FLAVEL.

God's rod, like Jonathan's, is dipped in honey.
—GEORGE SWINNOCK.

He that rides to be crowned will not think much of a rainy day.
—JOHN TRAPP.

Here is sweet fruit from a bitter stock.—THOMAS WATSON.

God and adversity will be good company.
—GEORGE SWINNOCK.

28 January

THE PROUD

Boasters, proud.—2 Tim. 3:2.
Highminded.—2 Tim. 3:4.

BLADDERS blown up with wind, will not lie close together, but prick them, and you may pack a thousand in a small space.—JOHN FLAVEL.

A proud heart eyes more his seeming worth than his real want.
—THOMAS BROOKS.

It is difficult to be high and not to be highminded.
—WILLIAM JENKYN.

Pride is intolerable to pride.—RICHARD SIBBES.

A proud heart always prizes himself above the market.
—THOMAS BROOKS.

Pride is no better an argument of an elect soul than a tumid swelling is of a sound body.—WILLIAM JENKYN.

Proud men surpass every kind of drunkenness.—JOHN CALVIN.

29 January

THEFT

If thieves come to thee, if robbers by night.—Obad. 5.

SOME will not want a fire if there be fuel in their neighbour's yard.—THOMAS FULLER.

Many build hospitals for children with their fathers' bones.
—WILLIAM JENKYN.

It is a wonder if old thieves be taken without an excuse.
—THOMAS FULLER.

Conquest is a cracked title.—WILLIAM GURNALL.

Many legacies which came sound forth from the testator, before they could get through the executors, have been more lame and maimed than the cripples in the hospital to whom they have been bequeathed.—THOMAS FULLER.

The civilest and best thief is but a thief.—THOMAS GRANGER.

He would be loath to have his own goods stolen that makes no conscience of robbing others.—THOMAS ADAMS.

30 January

FALSE HUMILITY

Priding himself on his humility.—Col. 2:18. (WEYMOUTH.)

HUMILITY itself is against humility, and by a strange prodigious birth brings forth pride.—THOMAS ADAMS.

He that brags of his humility loseth it.—JOHN BOYS.

He that carries grace in a proud heart carries dust in the wind.
—WILLIAM JENKYN.

Had pride been a weapon whereat a duel had been fought betwixt Alexander and Diogenes, probably the conqueror of the world had been worsted by a poor philosopher.
—THOMAS FULLER.

Many are humbled but not humble, low but not lowly.
—JOHN TRAPP.

The hypocrite hath a squint eye, for he looks more to his own glory than God's.—THOMAS WATSON.

31 JANUARY

CUSTOM

Ye have a custom.—John 18:39.
We have no such custom.—1 Cor. 11:16.
It was a custom in Israel.—Judg. 11:39.

CUSTOM is not only a grave to bury the soul in, but a stone rolled to the mouth of it to keep it down.
—THOMAS ADAMS.

When a custom is forthwith converted into a law, injustice is perpetrated.—JOHN CALVIN.

Custom without righteousness is but antiquity of iniquity.
—JOHN TRAPP.

Custom in sin takes away all conscience of sin.
—GEORGE SWINNOCK.

Long *nurture* is another *nature*.—THOMAS ADAMS.

People walk not in the best, but in the beaten way.
—JOHN BOYS.

That which is begun by an unjust title fortifies itself by custom.
—THOMAS ADAMS.

1 February

RAIN

The small rain upon the tender herb.—Deut. 32:2.
A sweeping rain which leaveth no food.—Prov. 28:3.

GOD, by the seasonable weeping of the heaven, hath caused the plentiful laughter of the earth.—THOMAS FULLER.

Moderate showers refresh the earth, immoderate drown it.
—WILLIAM JENKYN.

When the thunder shakes the air, the clouds weep to still it.
—THOMAS ADAMS.

Not a drop of rain falls in vain.—JOHN TRAPP.

The sweetest showers should fall on the lower grounds.
—GEORGE SWINNOCK.

That quantity of rain will make a clay ground drunk which will scarce quench the thirst of a sandy country.
—THOMAS FULLER.

Much rain is a burden to clouds, and much riches are a burden to men.—HENRY SMITH.

2 February

GOD NOT AUTHOR OF SIN

Is there unrighteousness with God? God forbid.—Rom. 9:14.
Is … Christ the minister of sin? God forbid.—Gal. 2:17.

OUR motion is from God, but not the disorder of that motion.—STEPHEN CHARNOCK.

He formed this crooked serpent [Satan] though not the crookedness of this serpent.—RICHARD BAXTER.

God sent corn and the devil sent garners.—NEHEMIAH ROGERS.

The sun and earth are not the cause of that poison which is in the nature of the plant.—STEPHEN CHARNOCK.

Man's fault cannot prejudice God's right.—WILLIAM GURNALL.

God made the face, and the devil paints it.—THOMAS ADAMS.

We owe our creation to God, our corruption to ourselves.
—STEPHEN CHARNOCK.

3 February

JUSTICE

The justice of the Lord.—Deut. 33:21
My justice was as a robe and a diadem.—Job 29:14. (R.V.)

THE judge of the earth keepeth his petty-sessions now, letting the law pass upon some few, reserving the rest till the great assizes.—JOHN TRAPP.

His will is the rule of righteousness, and righteousness is the rule of his will.—ELISHA COLES.

Pride cannot sit so high but Justice will sit above her.
—THOMAS BROOKS.

Justice would not be justice if it used not them with the greatest severity that abuse grace with the greatest indignity.
—STEPHEN CHARNOCK.

Without justice, great commonwealths are but great troops of robbers.—JOHN OWEN.

Justice in rigour is oft extreme injustice.—RICHARD STOCK.

A judge must not sit to hear *persons* but *causes*; therefore justice is drawn blindfold.—JOHN TRAPP.

4 February

PEDIGREE, HEREDITY AND ANTIQUITY

We be Abraham's seed.—John 8:33.
Them of old time.—Matt. 5:33.

IF Abraham's faith be not in your hearts, it will be no advantage that Abraham's blood runs in your veins.—JOHN FLAVEL.

Our father was Adam, our grandfather dust, our great-grandfather nothing.—WILLIAM JENKYN.

The son is the father in a later and newer edition.
—GEORGE SWINNOCK.

Solomon had but one son, and he was none of the wisest.
—JOHN TRAPP.

Piety is the best parentage.—WILLIAM SECKER.

It is true nobility where God is the chief and top of the kin.
—JOSEPH CHURCH.

Iniquity can plead antiquity.—THOMAS ADAMS.

As water, the nearer the spring the purer the stream, so in antiquity in customs.—CHRISTOPHER NESSE.

5 February

FAITH

According to your faith be it unto you.—Matt. 9:29.
The measure of faith.—Rom. 12:3.

THE larger faith we bring, the larger measure we carry from Christ.—RICHARD SIBBES.

Let faith have the hindmost word.—DAVID DICKSON.

Here it is no matter how much milk or holy broth there is; but how big is thy bowl, thy faith. Our mess* must be according to our measure.—JOHN BUNYAN.

Thou canst not see Christ with another's eyes, nor walk to heaven with another's feet.—THOMAS ADAMS.

It is the *taking* a gift makes it the man's that takes it, and not the *offer* of it.—THOMAS GOODWIN.

Assure thyself thou hast a good measure of faith if thou feel want of faith.—JOHN BOYS.

Faith is the only receiving grace.—WILLIAM GURNALL.

---

* Mess = food.

6 February

THE VANITY OF WORLDLY HONOUR

*Haman told them of the glory of his riches ...
Yet all this availeth me nothing.*—Esth. 5:11, 13.

THE honourable garter cannot cure the gout, nor the chair of state ease the colic, nor a crown remove the headache.
—JOHN TRAPP.

All the honour and applause in the world is no better than an inheritance of wind, which the pilot is not sure of.
—STEPHEN CHARNOCK.

High seats are never but uneasy, and crowns themselves oft stuffed with thorns.—JOHN TRAPP.

Outward things will do no more good than a fair shoe to a gouty foot.—RICHARD SIBBES.

Glory fled from Saul who followed it, but followed David who fled from it.—JOHN TRAPP.

It is both meat and drink for a formalist to fast if others do but see it.—WILLIAM SECKER.

7 February

SUPERSTITION

I perceive that in all things ye are too superstitious.—Acts 17:22.

WOOD is not more ready to be set on fire than we are to follow superstition.—JOHN CALVIN.

Let us not superstitiously feign that the ghosts of those ceremonies may still walk, which long since were buried in Christ's grave.—THOMAS FULLER.

That blind goddess Fortune holds her deity only by the tenure of man's ignorance.—WILLIAM JENKYN.

Fortune is but the devil's blasphemous spit upon divine providence.—CHRISTOPHER NESSE.

The best gamester hath commonly the worst luck.
—THOMAS GOODWIN.

Superstition is nothing else but an unscriptural and unrevealed dread of God.—STEPHEN CHARNOCK.

Superstition is more tolerable than that gross impiety which obliterates every thought of a God.—JOHN CALVIN.

8 February

EVIL CONSCIENCE

Conscience seared with a hot iron.—1 Tim. 4:2.
An evil conscience.—Heb. 10:22.

ONE small drop of an evil conscience troubleth a whole sea of outward comforts.—JOHN TRAPP.

A par-boiled conscience is not right, soft in one part and hard in another.—WILLIAM GURNALL.

God doth not usually bless with peace of conscience such as make no conscience of peace.—JOHN FLAVEL.

Some serve their consciences as David did Uriah; make it drunk that they may be rid of it.—GEORGE SWINNOCK.

While conscience holds the whip over them many will pray.
—JOSEPH ALLEINE.

That man can never have good days that keeps an evil conscience.—BENJAMIN KEACH.

There is more hope of a *sore* than of a *seared* conscience.
—JOHN TRAPP.

9 February

GOODNESS OF THE SAINTS

I myself also am persuaded of you, my brethren, that ye yourselves are full of goodness.—Rom. 15:14. (R.V.)

TRUE goodness is public-spirited, though to private disadvantage.—JOHN TRAPP.

He was never good that mends not.—GEORGE SWINNOCK.

If I cease becoming better I shall soon cease to be good.
—OLIVER CROMWELL.

No man can love a saint as a saint but a saint.
—RICHARD SIBBES.

True piety hath true plenty.—GEORGE SWINNOCK.

Let the Pope's calendar only saint the dead, the Scripture requires sanctity in the living.—WILLIAM JENKYN.

Sanctity is no enemy to courtesy.—JOHN TRAPP.

10 February

IDLE PRAYER

When thou prayest, thou shalt not …—Matt. 6:5.

THE prayer that wants a good aim wants a good issue.
—THOMAS WATSON.

Cold prayers shall never have any warm answers.
—THOMAS BROOKS.

Where God hath not a mouth to speak, men must not have a tongue to ask.—CHRISTOPHER NESSE.

Nature's praying is a pool that will dry up in a long drought.
—THOMAS BOSTON.

Cold prayers, like cold suitors, never speed.—THOMAS WATSON.

He which giveth God his lips instead of his heart, teacheth God to give him stones instead of bread.— HENRY SMITH.

Cold prayers always freeze before they reach heaven.
—THOMAS BROOKS.

The prayer that is faithless is fruitless.—THOMAS WATSON.

11 February

THE GOSPEL

The everlasting gospel.—Rev. 14:6.

THE gospel was of an eternal resolution, though of a temporary revelation.—STEPHEN CHARNOCK.

The gospel is an anvil that has broken many a hammer, and will break many hammers yet.—JOHN CALVIN.

The gospel is called grace because it publisheth, offers, and applies grace.—RICHARD SIBBES.

The waters of the sanctuary run only through the channels of the gospel.—STEPHEN CHARNOCK.

No softening like gospel-softening, no hardening like gospel-hardening.—GEORGE SWINNOCK.

The thunder of the gospel made Satan fall like lightning.
—JOHN CALVIN.

Spirituality is the genius of the gospel.—STEPHEN CHARNOCK.

12 February

AMBITION

Then Adonijah the son of Haggith exalted himself, saying, I will be king.—1 Kings 1:5.
Diotrephes, who loveth to have the preeminence.—3 John 9.

AMBITION, like the crocodile, groweth while it liveth.
—JOHN TRAPP.

Ambition, like the grave, is never full.—THOMAS ADAMS.

'Who am I?' saith Moses. 'Who am I not?' saith our upstart.
—JOHN BOYS.

Some climb so high that they break their necks.
—GEORGE SWINNOCK.

Ambition is so great a planet that it must have a whole orbit to move in.—WILLIAM SECKER.

Ambition rideth without reins.—JOHN TRAPP.

There is no scab or itch more dangerous than the ambition of sects and new opinions.—NEHEMIAH ROGERS.

Empty spirits affect swelling titles.—JOHN TRAPP.

13 FEBRUARY

SIN IN THE BEST

David did ... right in the eyes of the Lord ... all the days of his life, save only in the matter of Uriah the Hittite.—1 Kings 15:5.

IF the best man's faults were written in his forehead, it would make him pull his hat over his eyes.—JOHN TRAPP.

As long as there are spots in the moon, it is vain to expect anything spotless under it.—THOMAS FULLER.

Sin in a Christian is like a diver's dress on land, awkward and harassing.—JOHN TRAPP.

Spots are sooner seen in scarlet than in sackcloth.
—GEORGE SWINNOCK.

As the moon hath her specks, so the best have their blemishes.
—JOHN TRAPP.

The best saints in this world are like the tribe of Manasses: half on this side Jordan, and half on that.—THOMAS BROOKS.

The finest garment is soonest stained.—HENRY SMITH.

As in a fish, so in a church and state, corruption begins at the head.—JOHN TRAPP.

14 February

PREVENTION IS BETTER THAN CURE

Ye should have hearkened unto me, and not have set sail from Crete, and have gotten this injury and loss.—Acts 27:21. (R.V.)

IT is more easy to *exclude* sin than to *expel* it.
—THOMAS ADAMS.

To keep an enemy from rising is much easier than to quell him when he is up.—ELISHA COLES.

When the hem is worn the whole garment will ravel out, if that be not mended by timely repentance.

It is better to be innocent than penitent.—WILLIAM SECKER.

It is easier carrying provision to sea than getting it there.
—WILLIAM GURNALL.

It is easier for a bird to go by the net than to break the net.
—HENRY SMITH.

In God's temple have more of Sabbath thoughts on week-day, then week-day thoughts will less trouble you on Sabbath-day.—CHRISTOPHER NESSE.

15 February

MERCY

He delighteth in mercy.—Mic. 7:18.

WITHOUT faith we are not fit to desire mercy, without humility we are not fit to receive it, without affection we are not fit to value it, without sincerity we are not fit to improve it.—STEPHEN CHARNOCK.

There is no reason to be given for mercy, but mercy.
—RALPH VENNING.

Thou standest in a centre, the circumference is mercy.
—NEHEMIAH ROGERS.

Shall there be more mercy in the stream than in the spring?
—RICHARD SIBBES.

He that hath enough mercy can want nothing.—JOHN BOYS.

One ray of mercy is better than a sun of pleasure.
—WILLIAM SECKER.

Mercy's clock does not strike at the sinner's beck.
—THOMAS WATSON.

The bow smites not all it threatens.—CHRISTOPHER NESSE.

God is not merciful as a flint yields fire, by force, but as a spring whence water naturally issues.—RICHARD SIBBES.

16 February

PRIDE AND OTHER SINS

Pride hath budded.—Ezek. 7:10.
Pride, and arrogancy, and the evil way, and the froward mouth.
—Prov. 8:13.

PRIDE is the root of passion; a lofty will be a surly spirit.

Pride is a sin that will put the soul upon the worst of sins.
—THOMAS BROOKS.

Pride is the shirt of the soul, put on first and put off last.
—GEORGE SWINNOCK.

Pride is the very image of the devil.—THOMAS BOSTON.

The wind of pride is the life and soul of error; it is the element in which it moves and breathes.—WILLIAM JENKYN.

The worm of pride breeds soonest in rotten wood.
—GEORGE SWINNOCK.

Spiritual pride is a white devil.—THOMAS BROOKS.

Arrogancy is a weed that ever groweth in dung-hills.
—GEORGE SWINNOCK.

17 February

JUST ANGER

Be ye angry, and sin not.—Eph. 4:26.
He ... looked round about on them with anger.—Mark 3:5.
I was very angry.—Neh 5:6.

HE that will be angry and not sin, must not be angry but for sin.—JOHN TRAPP.

Anger should not be destroyed but sanctified.
—WILLIAM JENKYN.

'Be angry and sin not', is, saith one, the easiest charge under the hardest condition.—JOHN TRAPP.

Be soonest angry with thyself.—THOMAS FULLER.

It is not a sin to be angry, but hard not to sin when we are angry.—JOHN TRAPP.

Plato said to his servant, 'I would have killed thee, but that I am angry.'—JOHN KING.

Anger may *rush* into a wise man's bosom, but should not *rest* there.—JOHN TRAPP.

18 February

MIND

Lean not unto thine own understanding.—Prov. 3:5.
Sober minded.—Titus 2:6.

OUR understandings are so bad that they understand not their own business.—THOMAS FULLER.

The mind of man is much wider than his mouth.
—GEORGE SWINNOCK.

Our greatest sins are those of the mind.—THOMAS GOODWIN.

Our minds are as ill-set as our eyes; neither of them look inwards.—JOHN TRAPP.

The mind, like the ark, should be the chest of the law.
—THOMAS MANTON.

How often are poor Christians in danger of losing the eyes of their mind by those of their body.—JOHN FLAVEL.

Our minds are a beam from God.—STEPHEN CHARNOCK.

19 February

EXAMPLE—GOOD AND BAD

Walk even as ye have us for an ensample.—Phil. 3:17. (R.V.)
Look on me, and do likewise.—Judg. 7:17.

GREAT men are the looking-glasses of their country; according to which most men dress themselves.—JOHN TRAPP.

If both horse and mare trot, the colt will not amble.
—JOHN BOYS.

Old Testament examples are New Testament instructions.
—JOHN OWEN.

Example is the most powerful rhetoric.—THOMAS BROOKS.

No marvel the imps do follow when the devil goeth before.
—HENRY SMITH.

However ridiculous soever a garb appears, fashion can persuade men to it.—THOMAS ADAMS.

When princes are fiddlers, the people turn dancers.
—JOHN BOYS.

20 February

GOD—LIGHT, LOVE AND SPIRIT

God is light.— 1 John 1:5.
God is love.—1 John 4:8.
God is ... spirit.—John 4:24.

THE love of God is like a sea, into which when a man is cast, he neither seeth bank, nor feeleth bottom.—JOHN BOYS.

Love was a god among the heathen; God is love, saith the Christian.—THOMAS ADAMS.

God doth not know creatures because they are, but they are because he knows them.—STEPHEN CHARNOCK.

God is not wasted by bestowing.—THOMAS MANTON.

It is visible *that* God is, it is invisible *what* he is.
—STEPHEN CHARNOCK.

God hath the wisdom of a father, but he hath the bowels* of a mother.—RICHARD SIBBES.

The sense of our Father's love is like honey at the end of every rod.—TIMOTHY CRUSO.

FAITH AND HOPE

* The compassionate heart.

21 February

Faith and hope.—1 Pet. 1:21.

FAITH looks to the word promising, hope to the things promised in the word.—RICHARD SIBBES.

Hope is never ill when faith is well.—JOHN BUNYAN.

Faith regards the word of the substance, and hope the substance of the word.—THOMAS ADAMS.

Trust is nothing else but the strength of hope.
—RICHARD SIBBES.

If faith did not feed the lamp of hope with oil it would soon die.—THOMAS WATSON.

What trust believes by faith, it waits for by hope.
—ROBERT MOSSOM.

Faith comes by hearing, hope by experience. Faith fights for doctrine, hope for a reward.—JOHN BUNYAN.

The nature of hope is to expect that which faith believes.
—RICHARD SIBBES.

22 February

PRESUMPTION

The soul that doeth ... presumptuously ... shall be cut off.
—Num. 15:30.
And thou saidst, I shall be a lady for ever.—Isa. 47:7.
Turning the grace of our God into lasciviousness.—Jude 4.
I sit a queen ... and shall see no sorrow. —Rev. 18:7.

NO poison so deadly as that which is extracted out of grace.—WILLIAM JENKYN.

He that sins because of mercy is like one that wounds his head because he hath a plaster.—THOMAS WATSON.

Gather not wild gourds a second time (2 Kings 4:39), lest your prophet be absent or meal denied you.—ELISHA COLES.

Whom oil and balsam kill, what salve can cure?
—GEORGE HERBERT.

A man may be so bold of his predestination that he forget his conversation.*—THOMAS ADAMS.

It is not for every private soldier on every danger to make judgment of the battle.—JOHN OWEN.

---

* Manner or way of life.

23 FEBRUARY

FLESH AND SPIRIT

*That which is born of the flesh is flesh;
and that which is born of the Spirit is spirit.*—John 3:6.
The flesh lusteth against the Spirit.—Gal. 5:17.

EVERY faithful man's bosom is a Rebecca's womb wherein there are twins; a rough Esau and the seed of promise, the old man and the new.—JOSEPH HALL.

Satan hath a spite against the new creature.—THOMAS WATSON.

Beware of those enchanting sirens, flesh and blood.
—JOHN RAINOLDS.

The flesh is a wily servant, and will lie, like Gehazi, to his master.—HENRY SMITH.

The flesh is least contented when it is most satisfied.
—JOHN BOYS.

The mortification of the flesh is the quickening of the spirit.
—JOHN CALVIN.

A mite of spirit is of more worth than a mountain of flesh.
—STEPHEN CHARNOCK.

24 February

JUSTICE AND MERCY

Plenty of justice.—Job 37:23.
Plenteous in mercy.—Psa. 103:8.
A just God and a Saviour.—Isa. 45:21.

MERCY is 'Alpha', justice is 'Omega'.—THOMAS BROOKS.

Justice requires that there should be desert,[*] but mercy looks upon them that are miserable.—RICHARD STOCK.

Justice will take up the quarrel of abused mercy.
—THOMAS MANTON.

God hath two hands, a right hand of mercy and a left hand of justice.—JOHN BOYS.

Justice always makes mercy dumb, when sin has made the sinner deaf.—THOMAS BROOKS.

Necessity should have the most law, because she hath the least money.—HENRY SMITH.

All the rejoicing we have against God's justice is in the victory of his mercy.—THOMAS MANTON.

---

[*] Deserving, merit.

25 February

WORSHIP

Worship the Father in spirit and in truth: for the Father seeketh such to worship him.—John 4:23.

THE nature of God is the foundation of worship, the will of God is the rule of worship.—STEPHEN CHARNOCK.

Posture in worship is too often imposture.—THOMAS WATSON.

With the Spirit it is better, like Jonah, to be praying in a whale's belly, than without the Spirit to be devout in a gilded chapel.—WILLIAM JENKYN.

It is a poor worship to move our hats, not our hearts.
—THOMAS ADAMS.

The first foundation of righteousness undoubtedly is the worship of God.—JOHN CALVIN.

God is glorified only by being made known.
—THOMAS GOODWIN.

God is most exalted with fewest words.
—ALEXANDER CARMICHAEL.

The more exalted pomp there be of men's devising, there will be the less spiritual truth.—GEORGE HUTCHESON.

26 February

APOSTASY

A falling away.—2 Thess. 2:3.

APOSTASY is a perversion to evil after a seeming conversion from it.—TIMOTHY CRUSO.

Whatsoever doth begin in hypocrisy will end in apostasy.
—RICHARD SIBBES.

No vinegar so tart as that which is made from the sweetest wine.—THOMAS MANTON.

Infidelity is the mother of apostasy.—JOHN TRAPP.

He that staggers is next door to apostasy.—WILLIAM GURNALL.

It had better not to have known the way of truth, than not to persist in it.—JOHN KING.

Indifference in religion is the first step to apostasy from religion.
—WILLIAM SECKER.

A stop in knowledge is the first inlet to apostasy.
—STEPHEN CHARNOCK.

27 February

CHASTENING AND SONSHIP

If ye endure chastening, God dealeth with you as with sons.—Heb. 12:7.
Chastisement, whereof all are partakers.—Heb. 12:8.

AFFLICTION is a badge of adoption.—THOMAS WATSON.

The Lord uses his flail of tribulation to separate the chaff from the wheat.—JOHN BUNYAN.

A Christian's life can no more be *sine luctibus*, than the sea *sine fluctibus*.*—THOMAS ADAMS.

One son God hath without sin, but none without sorrow.
—JOHN TRAPP.

It is chaff that flieth in the face of him that fanneth.
—WILLIAM JENKYN.

Job was a non-such† for sanctity, yet full of sores.
—GEORGE SWINNOCK.

Better ragged saint than robed sinner.—WILLIAM GURNALL.

He that escapes affliction may well suspect his adoption.
—JOHN TRAPP.

---

* *Sine luctibus* = without sorrows; *sine fluctibus* = without waves.
† Unique, unparalleled, extraordinary.

28 FEBRUARY

THE DEVIL'S CAPTIVES

Taken captive by [the devil] at his will.—2 Tim. 2:26.

THE sinner's heart is the devil's mansion house.
—THOMAS WATSON.

Where Satan hath dwelt long, he will hardly be removed.
—GEORGE SWINNOCK.

The devil is the merchant, and the sinner the broker to trade for him.—WILLIAM GURNALL.

He that saith Yea to the devil in a little, shall not say Nay when he pleases.—JOHN TRAPP.

The proud man is Satan's throne and the idle man his pillow.
—GEORGE SWINNOCK.

Some men's heads are the devil's mint-house, they are a mint of mischief.—THOMAS WATSON.

Those that want legs to go in goodness, can find wings to fly in wickedness.—THOMAS FULLER.

29 February

THERE MAY BE ...

There may be ...—Exod. 7:19; Mal. 3:10; 2 Cor. 8:14.

THERE may be a trust in God where there is a walk in darkness.—STEPHEN CHARNOCK.

There may be gaudy signs at the door where there is not a drop of good wine in the cellar.—GEORGE SWINNOCK.

There may be joy *in* God when there is little joy *from* God.
—STEPHEN CHARNOCK.

There may be a time when God will not be found, but no time wherein he must not be trusted.—THOMAS LYE.

There may be a joy in a title as well as in possession.
—STEPHEN CHARNOCK.

There may be a clear head without a clean heart
—GEORGE SWINNOCK.

There may be gold in the mine when no flowers on the surface.—STEPHEN CHARNOCK.

There may be a ruffling the fringe in circumstantials where there is no rending the garment in substantials.
—CHRISTOPHER NESSE.

1 March

HASTE

He that believeth shall not make haste.—Isa. 28:16.
Be not rash with thy mouth, and let not thine heart be hasty.
—Eccles. 5:2.

THE best that can come of rashness is repentance.
—JOHN TRAPP.

Rush is destructive of rest, and pace of peace.
—THOMAS ADAMS.

Devotion without discretion is like a hasty servant that runs away without his errand.—THOMAS ADAMS.

Herod, by reason of a rash oath, cast himself into a worse prison than that wherein he had put the Baptist.
—THOMAS FULLER.

It is no pain to tarry for that which shall not fail us.
—EDWARD MARBURY.

The emptiest men are the most rash.—RICHARD SIBBES.

Hasty births do not fill the house but the grave.
—THOMAS MANTON.

Hasty men, we say, never want woe.—JOHN TRAPP.

2 March

VOWS AND SWEARING

When thou vowest a vow unto God, defer not to pay it.—Eccles. 5:4.

THAT which a promise is to men, that a vow is to God.
—RICHARD SIBBES.

One vow made and kept after the tempest is worth a thousand promised in the same.—THOMAS FULLER.

The most inviolable of our vows is that which binds us to the obedience of God.—JEAN DAILLÉ.

Swear not in jest, lest you go to hell in earnest.—JOHN TRAPP.

Peter forgot his Master and then forgot himself.
—WILLIAM JENKYN.

The life of an honest man is an oath.—RICHARD SIBBES.

Better to bear than to swear, and to die than to lie.
—THOMAS BROOKS.

Cursing men are cursed men.—JOHN TRAPP.

3 March

HEAVEN AND SIN

There shall in no wise enter into it any thing that defileth.
—Rev. 21:27.

HE that keeps earth by wrong cannot expect heaven by right.—WILLIAM GURNALL.

They who are not made saints in a state of grace shall never be saints in glory.—ROBERT LEIGHTON.

Heaven begins where sin ends.—THOMAS ADAMS.

In heaven they may find the want of evil, but never feel the evil of want.—EDWARD WILLAN.

If Christ be not the foundation of our perfection on earth, he will not be the topstone of our salvation in heaven.
—WILLIAM SECKER.

No one shall be kept out of heaven but such as love the world better than heaven.—HENRY SMITH.

Some would have heaven, but if God save them, he must save their sins also, for they do not mean to part with them.
—WILLIAM GURNALL.

4 March

TRUE PREACHERS AND MINISTERS

I am appointed a preacher.—2 Tim. 1:11.
A good minister of Jesus Christ.—1 Tim. 4:6.
A minister of holy things.—Heb. 8:2. (R.V. Margin.)

HE doth preach most that doth live best.—JOHN BOYS.

A sleepy preacher cannot expect a waking auditory.
—WILLIAM JENKYN.

Make not that wearisome that should ever be welcome.
—THOMAS FULLER.

Three things make a preacher: reading, prayer, and temptation.—JOHN TRAPP.

The doctrine of a minister must credit his life, and his life adorn his doctrine.—JEAN DAILLÉ.

If I were to choose my calling, I would dig with my hands rather than be a minister.—MARTIN LUTHER.

A pastor must thunder in his doctrine and lighten in his life.
—GEORGE SWINNOCK.

God had but one Son in the world, and he made him a minister.
—THOMAS GOODWIN.

5 MARCH

GOD'S PROTECTION AND RESTRAINT OF US

Thy rod and thy staff they comfort me. [The rod to protect from wild beasts and the staff to restrain from wandering.]—Psa. 23:4.

THERE is a twofold hedge that God makes about his people: there is the hedge of protection, to keep evil from them; and the hedge of affliction, to keep them from evil.
—JOHN BUNYAN.

If the command of God be not a hedge to keep thee from being a straying sheep, his care shall be no hedge to keep thee from being a devoured sheep.—WILLIAM JENKYN.

Faith, the guide to keep us from desperation; love, the rule to keep us from presumption.—JOHN KING.

If you abstract fear from joy, joy will become light and wanton; and if you abstract joy from fear, fear then will become slavish.—WILLIAM BATES.

The Christian, like a net, must have both the lead of a godly fear, and the cork of a lively faith.—GEORGE SWINNOCK.

6 March

SIN SPARED AND DEFENDED

The people took of the spoil ... which should have been utterly destroyed.—1 Sam. 15:21.

I forced myself therefore, and offered the burnt offering.
—1 Sam. 13:12. (R.V.)

A HYPOCRITE ever leaves the devil some nest-egg to sit upon, though he take many away.—GEORGE SWINNOCK.

Herod would have a gap for his incest.—THOMAS WATSON.

The sparing of our sin is a sure argument thou art not truly humbled for any sin.—JOHN FLAVEL.

A sin is two sins when it is defended.—HENRY SMITH.

He may come to suffer for the treason, who harbours and abetteth the traitor.—GEORGE SWINNOCK.

Only to refrain evil is to be evil still.—THOMAS ADAMS.

Sin is never complete until it is excused.—HENRY SMITH.

7 March

SYMPATHY

And there appeared in the cherubim the form of a man's hand under their wings.—Ezek. 10:8.

I sat where they sat.—Ezek. 3:15.

I have you in my heart.—Phil. 1:7.

IT is good manners to be an unbidden guest at a house of mourning.—GEORGE SWINNOCK.

He that pincheth the little toe paineth the whole body.
—THOMAS FULLER.

Charcoal quickly kindles because it hath been in the fire.
—JOHN TRAPP.

Sympathy is a debt we owe to sufferers.—WILLIAM SECKER.

Love to ourselves is the pattern that we ought to walk by in loving others.—JAMES DURHAM.

He [a Christian] is not as a wooden leg, senseless of the other members' sufferings.—GEORGE SWINNOCK.

It should be between a strong saint and a weak as it is between two lute-strings that are tuned to another; no sooner one is struck but the other trembles.—THOMAS BROOKS.

8 March

OVERMUCH TALK

Should a man full of talk be justified?—Job 11:2.
In the multitude of words there wanteth not sin.—Prov. 10:19.

LOQUACITY hath ever been a note of folly.
—THOMAS ADAMS.

The least wit yields the most words.—JOHN TRAPP.

The spaniel loses the prey by barking at the game.
—WILLIAM SECKER.

Thou mayest esteem a man of many words and many lies much alike.—THOMAS FULLER.

In a thousand talents of worldly words a man shall hardly find an hundred pence of spiritual and heavenly wisdom, scarcely ten half-pence.—JOHN RING.

This conceit, that people have divinity when they can talk of it, is a very destructive conceit.—RICHARD SIBBES.

Error hath always most words.—THOMAS ADAMS.

Better to be like such heretics as do nothing else but pray, than to be such schismatics as do nothing else but prate.
—JOHN BOYS.

9 March

APOSTLES, PROPHETS AND EVANGELISTS

And he gave some, apostles; and some, prophets;
and some, evangelists.—Eph. 4:11.
First apostles, secondarily prophets.—1 Cor. 12:28.
Do the work of an evangelist.—2 Tim. 4:5.

ST PETER was an apostle, but not an evangelist; St Luke was an evangelist, but not an apostle; St Matthew was both an evangelist and an apostle, but not a prophet; but our St John was all these; in his epistles an apostle, in his apocalypse a prophet, in compiling his gospel an evangelist.—JOHN BOYS.

The prophets were legal apostles, the apostles were evangelical prophets.—THOMAS ADAMS.

As religion hath its gospel and evangelists, so hath irreligion too.—JOHN HOWE.

Fathers must not be preferred before apostles.
—STEPHEN CHARNOCK.

All are not apostles, yet all are ambassadors.—JAMES DURHAM.

10 March

PERSEVERANCE

Thou shouldest have smitten five or six times.—2 Kings 13:19.
Patient continuance in well doing.—Rom. 2:7.
Watching thereunto with all perseverance.—Eph. 6:18.

PERSEVERANCE is the sister of patience, the daughter of constancy, the mother of peace, the mistress of concord.
—THOMAS ADAMS.

He who gives over never truly began.—WILLIAM JENKYN.

It is the constant pace that goes furthest and freest from being tired.—THOMAS FULLER.

Waiting is a permanent continuance in the performance of duties against all difficulties and discouragements.
—JOHN OWEN.

One clapper will wear out divers bells.—THOMAS ADAMS.

All virtues run in the race; one only receiveth the garland – the image of most happy eternity – happy continuance.
—JOHN KING.

11 March

FAITH, DOUBTS, AND UNBELIEF

Lord, I believe; help thou mine unbelief.—Mark 9:24.
O thou of little faith, wherefore didst thou doubt?—Matt. 14:31.

IF faith be a certain knowledge, then an uncertain opinion is unbelief.—STEPHEN CHARNOCK.

Faith doth the same against the devil that unbelief doth to God.—JOHN BUNYAN.

What the Jews believed in the Old Testament they rejected in the New.—STEPHEN CHARNOCK.

'If so be' is not a phrase fit to proceed from the mouth of faith.
—JOHN KING.

Doubting doth not imply a want of faith, but a weakness of faith.—STEPHEN CHARNOCK.

As our faith is never perfect, it follows that we are partly unbelievers.—JOHN CALVIN.

Waverings where faith is, are like the tossings of a ship fast at anchor.—STEPHEN CHARNOCK.

12 March

BODY AND SOUL

Both soul and body.—Matt. 10:28.

AS the man is more noble than the house he dwells in, so is the soul more noble than the body.—JOHN BUNYAN.

The body hath many garments, but the soul hath one.
—HENRY SMITH.

The soul pays a dear rent for the tenement it now lives in.
—JOHN FLAVEL.

By fasting the body learns to obey the soul; by praying the soul learns to command the body.—WILLIAM SECKER.

Some have their souls, as swine, for no other use than, as salt, to keep their bodies from putrefaction.—JOHN TRAPP.

The soul being a spirit conveys more to the body than the body can to it.—STEPHEN CHARNOCK.

The body is the prison of the soul.—JOHN CALVIN.

No suit of apparel is by God thought good enough for the soul, but that which is made by God himself, and that is that curious thing, the body.—WILLIAM SECKER.

13 March

GRACE AND NATURE

By nature the children of wrath.—Eph. 2:3.
By the grace of God I am what I am.—1 Cor. 15:10.

NATURE is content with little; grace with less.
—JOHN TRAPP.

Grace grows not upon the old stock.—STEPHEN CHARNOCK.

Nature without grace is as Samson without his guide, when his eyes were out.—JOHN KING.

The grace that hangs on by tacks like a mantle, soon drops off.—WILLIAM JENKYN.

The love of grace in another requires more than nature in ourselves.—JEAN DAILLÉ.

Nurture may somewhat amend nature, yet it is grace alone that can keep us within the bounds of obedience.—JOHN TRAPP.

Whatsoever is not above the top of nature is below the bottom of grace.—WILLIAM SECKER.

14 March

HYPOCRISY

Ye also outwardly appear righteous unto men, but within ye are full of hypocrisy and iniquity.—Matt. 23:28.

WHEN religion is in fashion, many will dress themselves by her looking-glass.—GEORGE SWINNOCK.

Hypocrisy is as like piety as hemlock to parsley, and many a one hath been deceived therein.—THOMAS FULLER.

Hypocrisy is a lie with a fair cover over it.—WILLIAM GURNALL.

Feigned equity is double iniquity.—GEORGE DOWNAME.

What greater falseness than to be in the skin a Christian and in the core a heathen.—WILLIAM JENKYN.

Silver looketh white and yet draweth black lines.
—GEORGE SWINNOCK.

It is a sad thing to be Christians at a supper, heathens in our shops, and devils in our closets.—STEPHEN CHARNOCK.

15 March

FAITH AND OTHER GRACES

Faith and love.—1 Tim. 1:14.
Faith and verity.—1 Tim. 2:7.
Faith and charity and holiness with sobriety.—1 Tim. 2:15.
Faith and patience.—Heb. 6:12.

FAITH is armour upon armour, a grace that preserves all the other graces.—WILLIAM GURNALL.

Faith hath an influence upon all other graces: it is like a silver thread that runs through a chain of pearls.
—THOMAS BROOKS.

Faith is the queen of the graces.—THOMAS WATSON.

Faith is the captain grace.—WILLIAM GURNALL.

Other graces make us like Christ, faith makes us members of Christ.—THOMAS WATSON.

All other graces, like birds in the nest, depend upon what faith brings in to them.—JOHN FLAVEL.

Faith is a file-leading grace.—WILLIAM GURNALL.

16 March

TEARS

Put thou my tears into thy bottle.—Psa. 56:8.

WHERE tears move not, nothing will move.
—HENRY SMITH.

Prayers and tears are the church's armour.—JOHN BOYS.

Sin brought in tears, and tears shall go away with sin.
—WILLIAM JENKYN.

No water so sweet as the saints' tears, when they do not overflow the banks of moderation.—THOMAS BROOKS.

Never did any man read his pardon with dry eyes.
—JOHN TRAPP.

If the white tears of God's servants be bottled up, surely the red tears are not cast away.—THOMAS FULLER.

You that have filled the book of God with your sins, should fill the bottle of God with your tears.—THOMAS GOODWIN.

Mary's tears were more precious to Christ than her ointment.
—THOMAS WATSON.

17 March

CHRIST THE HEAD

The head of every man is Christ.—1 Cor. 11:3.

LET all your senses have their seat in your head.
—ELISHA COLES.

Our heavenly head hath no staggering members.
—THOMAS ADAMS.

There is the same life in thy fingers and toes that there is in the head.—JOSEPH HALL.

Where should the tongue be but in the head?
—JOHN TRAPP.

A finger divorced from the hand receives no influence from the head.—WILLIAM SECKER.

Though Christ's coat was once divided, yet he will never suffer his crown to be divided.—THOMAS BROOKS.

It is a destructive addition to add anything to Christ.
—RICHARD SIBBES.

18 March

DRUNKENNESS

Be not drunk with wine, wherein is excess.—Eph. 5:18.

WHILE the wine is in thy hand, thou art a man; when it is in thine head, thou art become a beast.
—THOMAS ADAMS.

The drunkard is a walking quagmire.—WILLIAM JENKYN.

He that will never drink less than he may, sometimes will drink more than he should.—THOMAS FULLER.

Drunkenness is the metropolis of mischief.—JOHN TRAPP.

It is worse to live like a beast than to be a beast.
—WILLIAM GURNALL.

The drunkard is as dry as the sweating traveller.
—THOMAS ADAMS.

A drunkard's beastliness is his punishment as well as his sin.
—STEPHEN CHARNOCK.

The cup kills more than the cannon.—THOMAS WATSON.

19 March

UNFAITHFUL PREACHERS

My preaching was not with enticing words of man's wisdom.
—1 Cor. 2:4.

We are not fraudulent hucksters of God's message.
—2 Cor. 2:17. (WEYMOUTH.)

Concerning them that would lead you astray.—1 John 2:26. (R.V.)

THESE vain-glorious preachers may be like Rachel, fair, but their ministry is like to be barren.—WILLIAM GURNALL.

Once we had golden ministers and wooden vessels, now we have wooden ministers and golden vessels.—JOHN TRAPP.

The preaching that standeth not in relation to Christ is beside the text and mark.—JAMES DURHAM.

Those who sweat in worldly employments are commonly but cold in the pulpit.—WILLIAM JENKYN.

He that is more frequently in his pulpit *to* his people, than he is in his closet *for* his people, is but a sorry watchman.

—JOHN OWEN.

20 March

CONTRARIES

These are contrary the one to the other.—Gal. 5:17.

MUSIC and mourning agree like harp and harrow, like thin clothing and cold weather.—JOHN TRAPP.

Believers build their tombs where others build their tabernacles.
—WILLIAM SECKER.

He who is an enemy to a man's person will never be a friend to his precept.—GEORGE SWINNOCK.

God's wounds cure, sin's kisses kill.—WILLIAM GURNALL.

Contraries do expel one the other.—EDWARD MARBURY.

Though good ends make not bad actions lawful, yet bad ends make good actions sinful.—WILLIAM SECKER.

Contraries set near one another appear more visible.
—JAMES JANEWAY.

Sin is never at a higher flood than when grace is at a low ebb.
—THOMAS GOODWIN.

21 March

THE POWER AND WEAKNESS OF THE LAW OF GOD

By the law is the knowledge of sin.—Rom. 3:20.
What the law could not do.—Rom. 8:3.

THE law was a light, *lex est lux*.*—THOMAS ADAMS.

The law is the light and the commandment the lantern.
—WILLIAM AUSTIN.

The law may *express* sin but it cannot *suppress* sin.
—THOMAS ADAMS.

The Christian creed doth not vacate the ten commandments.
—WILLIAM GURNALL.

There is no death of sin without the death of Christ.
—JOHN OWEN.

The law, though it have no power to condemn us, hath power to command us.—THOMAS ADAMS.

God's fence is too low to keep a graceless heart in bounds when the game is before him.—WILLIAM GURNALL.

---

* *Lex est lux* = law is light.

22 March

REPENTANCE AND PARDON

Let the wicked forsake his way, and the unrighteous man his thoughts: and let him return unto the Lord, and he will have mercy upon him; and to our God, for he will abundantly pardon.—Isa. 55:7.

GOD will not pardon for repentance, nor yet without it.
—THOMAS WATSON.

Upon the two hinges of faith and repentance do all the saving promises of the Bible hang.—GEORGE SWINNOCK.

The Lord hath made a promise *to* late repentance, but where hath he made a promise *of* late repentance?
—THOMAS BROOKS.

That sin which is not too great to be forsaken, is not too great to be forgiven.—THOMAS HORTON.

Though God promise forgiveness to repenting sinners, yet God promiseth not tomorrow to repent in.
—GEORGE SWINNOCK.

All gospel mourning flows from believing.—THOMAS BROOKS.

23 March

UNION WITH CHRIST

I in them.—John 17:26.
Abide in me and I in you.—John 15:4.

TAKE away union and there can be no communion.
—JOHN FLAVEL.

Union is the ground of communion.—JOHN TRAPP.

Union with Christ entitles to all that is his.—ELISHA COLES.

Adam's sin hurts none but those that are in him, and Christ's blood profits none but those that are in him.—JOHN FLAVEL.

Every Christian quartereth arms with Christ.—JOHN TRAPP.

The nearer the union, the more dangerous the breach of it.
—WILLIAM SECKER.

The head in heaven cries out, 'Saul, Saul, why persecutest thou me?' when the toe was trod upon on earth.—JOHN FLAVEL.

24 March

BLINDNESS

Blind leaders of the blind.—Matt. 15:14.
The Philistines took him, and put out his eyes.—Judg. 16:21.

SAMSON was blind before he was blind.—THOMAS FULLER.

If the blind lead the blind, you know where to find them both.
—EDWARD MARBURY.

Sin always had deformity, but we had not always eyes to see it.
—WILLIAM JENKYN.

He that will be blind when he sins, shall be made wise when he suffers.—THOMAS ADAMS.

The blind leading the blind draws him not out of the puddle, but rather hurleth him in the ditch.—JOHN BOYS.

A blind eye is worse than a lame foot.—THOMAS WATSON.

Many make those eyes which God hath given them, as it were two lighted candles to let them see to go to hell.
—ARCHIBALD SYMSON.

25 March

HEARING AND ATTENTION

Give ear, O my people, to my law.—Psa. 78:1.

DRAW up the ears of your mind to the ears of your bodies that one sound may pierce both.—JOHN TRAPP.

Doers of the word are the best hearers.—THOMAS WATSON.

Attention of body, intention of mind, and retention of memory, are indispensably desired of all Wisdom's scholars.
—JOHN TRAPP.

The object cannot apply itself to the mind, but the mind must bring itself to the object.—NEHEMIAH ROGERS.

We can never hear that too often that we can never learn too well.—THOMAS BROOKS.

All in the church may hear the word of Christ, but few hear Christ in the word.—GEORGE SWINNOCK.

Unless God come in by the ear, you shall not find him in the heart.—THOMAS ADAMS.

26 March

SATAN AND SIN

The devil sinneth from the beginning.—1 John 3:8.
The devil having now put into the heart of Judas ... to betray him.
—John 13:2.

SIN was begotten in secret betwixt Satan and Eve.
—THOMAS ADAMS.

Every sin is an election of the devil to be our Lord.
—STEPHEN CHARNOCK.

Sin hath the devil for its father, shame for its companion, and death for its wages.—THOMAS WATSON.

The honour thou gettest by sin makes thee pensioner to the devil.—WILLIAM GURNALL.

If gluttony be the founder, Satan is the confounder.
—THOMAS ADAMS.

Have the devil for your taskmaster and you have him also for your paymaster.—JOHN TRAPP.

'Tis the crooked serpent brought men to crooked ways.
—CHRISTOPHER NESSE.

27 March

EXTREMES

Oppositions [lit. *antitheses*].—1 Tim. 6:20.

As the prodigal erreth in excess, so the niggard erreth in defect.—GEORGE SWINNOCK.

Cold diseases must have hot remedies.—RICHARD SIBBES.

There is sure a mean to be found betwixt *defying* men and *deifying* them.—WILLIAM GURNALL.

A Boanerges is as necessary as a Barnabas.—WILLIAM SECKER.

True love, like fire, burns hottest when the weather is coldest.
—GEORGE SWINNOCK.

Against every hill there is a dale.—THOMAS GOODWIN.

Gold in a dung-hill is more excellent than lead in a cabinet.
—THOMAS BROOKS.

The devil is always in extremes.—RICHARD SIBBES.

A mean scaffold may serve to rear up a goodly building.
—GEORGE SWINNOCK.

28 March

LAWYERS, PHYSICIANS, AND DIVINES

Zenas the lawyer.—Titus 3:13.
Luke, the beloved physician.—Col. 4:14.
John, the divine.—Rev. (Title.)

A LAWYER dying bequeathed all his goods to Bedlam; saying, Among madmen I got it, and let madmen spend it.—THOMAS ADAMS.

If the lots were cast to see who troubles the ship, it would fall upon the lawyers.—HENRY SMITH.

It is said of the surgeon that he must have a lady's hand and a lion's heart.—JOHN BOYS.

The physician saith, Nothing better for the body than abstinence; the divine saith, Nothing better for the soul than abstinence; the lawyer saith, Nothing better for the wits than abstinence.—HENRY SMITH.

In the lawyer's hands we lose but our goods; in the physician's hands but our life; but in the hands of a bad divine we may lose that which surpasseth all, our soul.—JOHN BOYS.

29 March
SHIRKING RESPONSIBILITY

I cast it into the fire, and there came out this calf.—Exod. 32:24.
As thy servant was busy here and there, he was gone.—1 Kings 20:40.

HE that will not bear the clapper must not pull the rope.
—JOHN FLAVEL.

To plead for sin is to be the devil's attorney.—THOMAS WATSON.

Sin and shifting came into the world together; never yet any came to hell, but had some pretence for coming hither.
—JOHN TRAPP.

Oh! that when a man saith, 'How can I forbear the bait?' he would ask himself, 'How can I endure the hook?'
—WILLIAM JENKYN.

Sin seldom wants a seeming reason.—RICHARD SIBBES.

He that hath promised and not performed is in worse case than he that never promised.—THOMAS ADAMS.

As the ostrich hath wings and flieth not, so some men have a calling but they answer it not.—ROBERT CAWDRAY.

30 March

FAITH WITHOUT WORKS

Faith, if it hath not works, is dead, being alone.—James 2:17.

NAKED faith is no faith.—THOMAS ADAMS.

A naked profession of faith is no better than a verbal charity.—THOMAS MANTON.

The want of good works makes faith sick; evil works kill her outright.—THOMAS ADAMS.

'Tis no wrong to good works to give faith the upper hand.
—THOMAS WATSON.

The eye alone sees, but not the eye that is alone, apart from the body.—WILLIAM JENKYN.

Faith is a great queen; it is base to let her go without a court and a train.—THOMAS ADAMS.

Faith believes as if it did not work, and it works as if it did not believe.—THOMAS WATSON.

31 March

THE CHURCH IN THE WORLD AND THE WORLD IN THE CHURCH

The saints ... that are of Caesar's household.—Phil. 4:22.
False brethren privily brought in.—Gal. 2:4. (R.V.)
He that feared the word of the Lord among the servants of Pharaoh.
—Exod. 9:20.

AS Christ hath his saints in Nero's court, so the devil his servants in the outer court of the visible church.
—WILLIAM GURNALL.

Doeg may set his foot as far within the tabernacle as David.
—JOHN TRAPP.

Everyone that hangs about the court does not speak with the king.—THOMAS WATSON.

Lot was the world's miracle, who kept himself fresh in Sodom's salt waters.—JOHN TRAPP.

The wheat and the chaff, they may both grow together but they shall not both lie together.—THOMAS GOODWIN.

Ishmael was an unbeliever in the house of faith.
—THOMAS ADAMS.

1 April

WIT, MIRTH, AND JESTING

A merry heart is a good medicine.—Prov. 17:22. (R.V.)
Foolish talking, or jesting ... are not befitting.—Eph. 5:4. (R.V.)

A MIND forestalled with levity is like a vessel without ballast, soon overset.—THOMAS ADAMS.

Wealth makes wit waver.—DAVID DICKSON.

Profane jests will come without calling.—THOMAS FULLER.

Be but wicked, and the devil will help thee to be witty.
—WILLIAM GURNALL.

That man pays too dear for a jest who sells his honesty for it.
—THOMAS ADAMS.

Wit unsanctified is a fit tool for the devil to work withal.
—JOHN TRAPP.

Harmless mirth is the best cordial against the consumption of the spirit.—THOMAS FULLER.

Pride commands the wit to justify anger.—RICHARD SIBBES.

2 April

ENVY

Then I saw all labour and every successful work, that for this a man is envied of his neighbour.—Eccles. 4:4. (R.V.)

Envy [is] the rottenness of the bones.—Prov. 14:30.

ENVY is its own punishment.—WILLIAM JENKYN.

Cain's envy hatched Abel's murder.—WILLIAM GURNALL.

Envy doth nothing with reason.—JOHN TRAPP.

Envy does ever ascend; it never descends.—THOMAS BROOKS.

As the dust cometh with the wind, so the devil cometh with envy.—HENRY SMITH.

Envy is a self-murder, a fretting canker.—THOMAS WATSON.

Other men's welfare is the envious man's wound.
—WILLIAM JENKYN.

Envy is a denial of providence.—STEPHEN CHARNOCK.

3 April

HOLY SCRIPTURE

The holy scriptures.—2 Tim. 3:15.

PLACES of Scripture are not to be taken by the tale but by the weight.—THOMAS FULLER.

In Scripture, every little daisy is a meadow.—MARTIN LUTHER.

Scripture is the spiritual glass to dress our souls by.
—THOMAS WATSON.

The same Testator made both Testaments.—THOMAS TAYLOR.

I would not live in paradise without the word, but with it I could make a shift to live in hell itself.—MARTIN LUTHER.

The two Testaments are the two lips by which God hath spoken to us.—THOMAS WATSON.

Till we are above sin, we are not above Scripture.
—THOMAS WATSON.

There is far more royal power in the thunder of the word, than in the word of thunder.—JOSEPH CARYL.

God's truth always agrees with itself.—RICHARD SIBBES.

4 April

THE FREQUENCY OF SLANDER

I have heard the slander of many.—Psa. 31:13.
We be slanderously reported.—Rom. 3:8.

EVERY public person had need to carry a spare handkerchief to wipe off the dirt and disgrace and obloquy cast upon him for doing his duty.—JOHN TRAPP.

Evil tongues are the devil's bellows.—JOHN TRAPP.

He that willingly takes from my good name, unwillingly adds to my reward.—THOMAS BROOKS.

He that cannot patiently bear reproaches and injuries may make up his pack, and get him out of the world; for here is no being for him.—JOHN TRAPP.

John Baptist's head in a charger is a usual dish at our meals.
—THOMAS MANTON.

If a wise man speak evil of thee, endure him; if a fool, pardon him.—JOHN TRAPP.

Those that have a mind to kill another man's dog make the world believe he was mad first.—JOHN TRAPP.

5 April

UNWORTHINESS

I am not worthy of the least of all the mercies ... which thou hast shewed unto thy servant.—Gen. 32:10.

I am not worthy that thou shouldest come under my roof.—Matt. 8:8.

IT is part of our worthiness to see our unworthiness.
—THOMAS WATSON.

The best qualification is to find yourself ill-qualified.
—ELISHA COLES.

No man begins to be good till he sees himself to be bad.
—THOMAS BROOKS.

Those are the best prepared for the greatest mercies that see themselves unworthy of the least.—THOMAS WATSON.

Self-emptiness prepares for spiritual fullness.—RICHARD SIBBES.

Christ dwells in that heart most eminently that hath emptied itself of itself.—THOMAS BROOKS.

God pours the golden oil of mercy into empty vessels.
—THOMAS WATSON.

6 April

APPEARANCES MAY DECEIVE

Man looketh on the outward appearance.—1 Sam. 16:7.
Judge not according to the appearance.—John 7:24.

A RUNNING sore may lie under a purple robe.
—STEPHEN CHARNOCK.

Heralds account the plainest coats the most ancient, better than those of a later edition, which are so full of filling that they are empty of honour.—THOMAS WATSON.

A man may wear Christ's livery and do the devil's drudgery.
—GEORGE SWINNOCK.

A wrinkled and deformed soul may dwell at the sign of a fair face.—THOMAS ADAMS.

Guests may be in the house when they look not out of the windows.—WILLIAM SECKER.

Sometimes a coward may dwell at the sign of a roaring voice and of a stern countenance.—SIMEON ASH.

7 April

COMMUNION

Enoch walked with God.—Gen. 5:22.
Noah walked with God.—Gen. 6:9.
Draw nigh to God, and he will draw nigh to you.—James 4:8.

ENOCH changed his place but not his company.
—JOHN TRAPP.

Likeness is the ground of communion.—STEPHEN CHARNOCK.

The true Christian is a closet man, he drives on a home-trade, a heart-trade.—JOHN FLAVEL.

Keep good neighbourhood to borrow and lend with Him.
—SAMUEL RUTHERFORD.

Next to communion with God is the communion of saints.
—JOHN TRAPP.

If there be two, he will be the third.—ALEXANDER PEDEN.

God breaks not with us till we break with him.
—STEPHEN CHARNOCK.

He is not a saint that seeketh not communion of saints.
—EDMUND CALAMY.

8 April

MEN GREAT AND SMALL

Small and great, rich and poor, free and bond.—Rev. 13:16.
God made ... great lights ... he made the stare also.—Gen. 1:16.

THE church is like a copse wherein the underwood grows much thicker and faster than the oaks.
—THOMAS FULLER.

Great men's vices are more imitated than poor men's graces.
—WILLIAM SECKER.

All Christ's scholars are not of the same form.
—GEORGE SWINNOCK.

All the house of Kish are not kings because Saul is one.
—THOMAS ADAMS.

There may be a greater distance between poor and poor than there is between poor and rich.—JOSEPH CARYL.

Shrubs may be grubbed to the ground and none miss them, but everyone marks the felling of a cedar.—THOMAS FULLER.

Every branch of the tree is not a top branch.
—MATTHEW HENRY.

9 April

ZEAL WITHOUT KNOWLEDGE

They have a zeal of God, but not according to knowledge.
—Rom. 10:2.

ZEAL without knowledge is like wild fire in a fool's hand.
—JOHN TRAPP.

As thy policy should not eat up thy zeal, so thy zeal must not eat up thy wisdom.—GEORGE SWINNOCK.

The heat of the fire cannot be made more intense without a supply of fuel.—STEPHEN CHARNOCK.

As wine is tempered with water, so let discretion temper zeal.
—HENRY SMITH.

Zeal to a Christian is like a high wind filling the sails of a ship, which, unless it be ballasted with discretion, doth but the sooner overturn it.—GEORGE SWINNOCK.

Zeal without discretion is like fire on the chimney-top; or like mettle in a blind horse; or the devil in the demoniac, that cast him sometimes into the fire and sometimes into the water.—JOHN TRAPP.

10 April

ARMOUR

Overcome evil with good.—Rom. 12:21.
All of them clothed in full armour.—Ezek. 38:4. (R.V.)
Wherefore take unto you the whole armour of God.—Eph. 6:13.

OUR enemies are on every side, so must our armour be.
—WILLIAM GURNALL.

A little might serve to defend a man if he might choose where his enemy should strike him.—JOHN OWEN.

Satan never beats us but with our own weapons.
—WILLIAM JENKYN.

We must not confide in the armour of God, but in the God of the armour.—WILLIAM GURNALL.

Every enemy insults over him that has lost the use of his weapons.—THOMAS BROOKS.

He makes a good market of bad commodities who, with kindnesses, overcomes injuries.—WILLIAM SECKER.

Our armour and our garments of flesh go off together.
—WILLIAM GURNALL.

11 April

THE BROKEN HEART

A broken and a contrite heart, O God, thou wilt not despise.
—Psa. 51:17.

THE broken heart is the only sound heart.—JOHN TRAPP.

He only that made the heart can mend it.

The Lord has two heavens to dwell in, and the holy heart is one of them.—THOMAS WATSON.

Other things may be the worse for breaking, yet a heart is never at the best till it be broken.—SIR RICHARD BAKER.

God can stop not only hands from spoiling, but hearts from desiring.—JOSEPH CARYL.

The seat of comfort is the seat of grief.—RICHARD SIBBES.

They that make their eyes a fountain to wash Christ's feet in shall have his side for a fountain to wash their souls in.
—JOHN TRAPP.

Concerning the heart God seems to say, as Joseph of Benjamin, if you bring not Benjamin with you, ye shall not see my face.—JOHN FLAVEL.

12 April

JUSTIFICATION, SANCTIFICATION, AND GLORIFICATION

But ye are justified.—1 Cor. 6:11.
Whom he justified, them he also glorified.—Rom. 8:30.

BY grace we are what we are in justification, and work what we work in sanctification.—RICHARD SIBBES.

Justification is blessedness begun; glorification blessedness perfected.—JOHN BOYS.

In proof of sanctification, good works cannot be sufficiently magnified; but in point of justification, good works cannot be sufficiently nullified.—WILLIAM SECKER.

God does not justify us because we are worthy, but by justifying us makes us worthy.—THOMAS WATSON.

Regeneration is the birth, sanctification is the growth of the babe in grace.—GEORGE SWINNOCK.

There is nothing destroyed by sanctification but that which would destroy us.—WILLIAM JENKYN.

13 April

MALICE

The leaven of malice.—1 Cor. 5:8.
Living in malice.—Titus 3:3.
Prating against us with malicious words.—3 John 10.

MALICE careth not how true the charge is, but how cutting.—JOHN TRAPP.

Charity begins with itself, malice with another.—JOHN BOYS.

Malice runs in the blood and, as we say of rennet,* the older it is the stronger.—JOHN TRAPP.

Malice is mental murder.—THOMAS WATSON.

Anger and malice differ but in age.—JOHN TRAPP.

Dislike soon spies a fault.—JOHN TRAPP.

Malice is an insatiable monster; it will minister words, as rage ministers weapons.—RICHARD SIBBES.

Malice cares not what it saith, so it may kill.—JOHN TRAPP.

---

* Rennet = curdled milk.

14 April

RELATIONSHIPS

My lovers and my friends ... and my kinsmen.—Psa. 38:11.
My mother and my brethren.—Luke 8:21.

THE virgin Mary, was more blessed in being the daughter, than in being the mother of Christ.—JOHN BOYS.

Mere neuters are no friends.—THOMAS GOODWIN.

He who refuses to be a son of the church in vain desires to have God as his Father.—JOHN CALVIN.

I have seen the twine-thread of a cordial friend hold, when the cable-rope of a rich kinsman hath broken.

—THOMAS FULLER.

Friendship with God makes enmity against Satan.

—JAMES JANEWAY.

Christ and faith are relatives which must not be severed.

—WILLIAM GURNALL.

The wicked are whelps of the same litter.—THOMAS GOODWIN.

A servant may use greater industry and pains than a son and yet please less.—THOMAS MANTON.

15 April

WHAT IS FAITH?

*Faith is the assurance of things hoped for,
the proving of things not seen.*—Heb. 11:1. (R.V.)

FAITH is the soul's ear.—JOHN BOYS.

Faith is not a distant view, but a warm embrace of Christ.
—JOHN CALVIN.

Faith is a stooping grace.—THOMAS WATSON.

Faith is the truest quench-coal to the fire of hell.
—ELISHA COLES.

Faith is the spear that killeth our last enemy.—JOHN BOYS.

Faith is your spiritual optic.—ELISHA COLES.

No such midwife as faith; it hath delivered even graves of their dead.—JOHN TRAPP.

Faith is a right pilgrim-grace; it travels with us to heaven, and when it sees us safe got within our Father's doors, it takes leave of us.—WILLIAM GURNALL.

It is the office of faith to believe what we do not see, and it shall be the reward of faith to see what we do believe.
—THOMAS ADAMS.

16 APRIL

DARKEST BEFORE DAWN

When Herod would have brought him forth, the same night ... behold, the angel of the Lord came.—Acts 12:6, 7.
From the horns of the wild-oxen thou hast answered me.
—Psa. 22:21. (R.V.)

'TIS a Jewish proverb, When the tale of bricks was doubled, then came Moses.—JOHN FLAVEL.

God reserveth his holy hand for a dead lift usually, and loveth to help those that are forsaken of their hopes.—JOHN TRAPP.

Water is at the lowest ebb before there is a spring-tide.
—THOMAS WATSON.

It mattered not though the ship be scanted of victuals when it is hard by the harbour.—THOMAS FULLER.

If there are no candles in the house, yet it is a comfort to think that it is almost day.—JOHN FLAVEL.

That was a dark night, when men went about to put out the sun which brought them light.—HENRY SMITH.

17 April

WISE REPROOF

And he made ... his snuffers ... of pure gold.—Exod. 37:23.
And of some have compassion, making a difference.—Jude 22.

IT is not for every fool to handle snuffers at or about the candles, lest perhaps, instead of mending the light, they put the candle out.—JOHN BUNYAN.

There is a difference to be put between an iron vessel and a Venice glass in the cleansing of them.—WILLIAM JENKYN.

Some warmth must be in a reproof but it must not be scalding hot.—JOHN TRAPP.

Some men's hearts are like nettles: touch them but gently and they will sting, when rough handling is without prejudice.—NEHEMIAH ROGERS.

Some men would receive blows with more patience if they were given them with more prudence.—GEORGE SWINNOCK.

A Venice glass is not to be rubbed so hard as a brazen kettle.
—WILLIAM SECKER.

18 April

SIN AND GRACE

Where sin abounded, grace did much more abound.—Rom. 5:20.

THOUGH sin and grace were never born together, and though they shall not die together, yet while the believer lives, these two must live together.—THOMAS BROOKS.

Grace sets up its ensigns in all parts of the soul, surveys every corner, and triumphs over every lurking enemy.
—STEPHEN CHARNOCK.

An interest in grace cannot consist with a known sin.
—THOMAS MANTON.

God's mercy can drown great sins, as the sea covers great rocks.
—THOMAS WATSON.

Grace found the richest saint but a beggarly sinner.
—WILLIAM JENKYN.

Grace is as large in renewing as sin was in defacing.
—STEPHEN CHARNOCK.

Sin and grace are like two buckets at a well: when one is up, the other is down.—THOMAS BROOKS.

19 April

BACKSLIDING

The backslider in heart shall be filled with his own ways.
—Prov. 14:14.
A perpetual backsliding.—Jer. 8:5.

A GARDEN once digged, and then let alone, becomes more weedy.—THOMAS ADAMS.

He falls deepest into hell who falls backward.
—THOMAS WATSON.

Weariness maketh way for wandering.—THOMAS MANTON.

None will have such a sad parting from Christ as those who went half-way with him and then left him.
—WILLIAM GURNALL.

Our committing sin will not speak us unsanctified, but our submitting to it will.—GEORGE SWINNOCK.

Miserable is that man who is beholden to the devil for his cordials.—JAMES JANEWAY.

The fidifragous* Christian speeds worse than the barbarous infidel.—THOMAS ADAMS.

---

* Fidifragous = unfaithful.

20 April

LIBERALITY AND MEANNESS

Being enriched in every thing to all liberality.—2 Cor. 9:11. (Margin.)
The churl.—Isa. 32:5.

CHARITY is the best way to plenty; he gets most that gives most.—GEORGE SWINNOCK.

Liberality is a fire which is maintained by thrift.
—THOMAS FULLER.

No man gives more than he that keepeth nothing back.
—THOMAS ADAMS.

Spare nothing that God may spare all.—RICHARD SIBBES.

He that lays up his gold may be a good jailer, but he that puts it out is a good steward.—FRANCIS RAWORTH.

Mercy is not miserly, charity is no churl.—JOHN TRAPP.

There is a good deal of copper faith in the world.
—THOMAS HOOKER.

I think you keep the rule of the gospel that the right hand knoweth not what the left doth, because neither right nor left doth anything.—JOHN KING.

21 April

OPPORTUNITY

A man of opportunity.—Lev. 16:21. (Margin.)
We have … opportunity.—Gal. 6:10.
Buying up the opportunity.—Col. 4:5. (R.V. Margin.)

OPPORTUNITY is the spirits of time extracted, or the quintessence of time at large distilled.—THOMAS FULLER.

Opportunities are for eternity, but not to eternity.
—WILLIAM SECKER.

Opportunity is headlong bald behind, having never a lock to catch hold of.—CHRISTOPHER NESSE.

Opportunity calleth us out to do many things we never intended.—THOMAS GRANGER.

Time is all the while a man liveth on the earth; but opportunity is only when the Spirit moveth.—GEORGE SWINNOCK.

He that neglects the occasion, the occasion will neglect him.
—JOHN FLAVEL.

God does not keep our time, because it is not the due time.
—THOMAS BOSTON.

22 April

HEAVEN AND HELL

Heaven is my throne.—Acts 7:49.
Flee from the wrath to come.—Matt. 3:7.
Cast ... down to hell.—2 Pet. 2:4.

HELL is the emphasis of misery.—THOMAS WATSON.

There is many a learned head in hell.—JOHN FLAVEL.

Ever is the hell of hell, so it is, the heaven of heaven.
—GEORGE SWINNOCK.

Hell is an abiding place, but no resting place.
—THOMAS WATSON.

Men might go to heaven with less trouble than they go to hell.—HENRY SMITH.

Hell is full of purposes, heaven of performances.
—JOHN ROGERS.

Many a man goes to hell in the sweat of his brow.
—THOMAS WATSON.

Hell is to be escaped by hearing.—CHRISTOPHER NESSE.

An idle person cannot find, either in heaven or hell, a pattern.
—GEORGE SWINNOCK.

23 April

CHASTENING

All chastening seemeth for the present to be not joyous, but grievous: yet afterward it yieldeth peaceable fruit unto them that have been exercised thereby.—Heb. 12:11. (R.V.)

AFFLICTIONS relish sour and bitter even to the palates of the best saints.—THOMAS FULLER.

We may feel God's hand as a Father upon us when he strikes us as well as when he strokes us.—ABRAHAM WRIGHT.

Correction may befall the saints but not destruction.
—THOMAS WATSON.

A righteous man may be corrected, albeit he is accepted of God.
—DAVID DICKSON.

Affliction is the whetstone of prayer and obedience.
—EDWARD MARBURY.

I had rather have God's vinegar than man's oil, God's wormwood than man's manna.—JOHN DONNE.

Bitter pills will down when made up in love.—THOMAS ADAMS.

24 APRIL

LIFE

For to him that is joined to all the living there is hope: for a living dog is better than a dead lion.—Eccles. 9:4.

LIFE is an excellency added to being.—THOMAS GOODWIN.

There is no going where there is no living.—JEAN DAILLÉ.

The life of our mortal life is the hope of an immortal.
—WILLIAM JENKYN.

A small tree is better than a great shadow.—THOMAS ADAMS.

The infant heir preferreth his milk before his largest manors.
—GEORGE SWINNOCK.

There never was one new-born who was still-born.
—WILLIAM SECKER.

Everything that generates, generates its like.—THOMAS BOSTON.

No divinity can be without life.—JOHN CALVIN.

25 April

THE GROWTH OF SIN

The woman saw ... she took ... and did eat, and gave also unto her husband.—Gen. 3:6.

I saw ... then I coveted them, and took them; ... they are hid ... in the midst of my tent.—Josh. 7:21.

THE beginnings of sin are modest, the progress adventurous, the conclusion may be impudent in open apostasy.
—WILLIAM JENKYN.

Sin is like the Jerusalem artichoke: plant it were you will, it overruns the ground, and chokes the heart.—JOHN TRAPP.

A sin of infirmity may admit apology; a sin of ignorance may find out excuse; but a sin of defiance can find no defence.
—SIR RICHARD BAKER.

Looking begat lusting. Intemperance begins at the eye.
—THOMAS WATSON.

One sin liked and loved will make way for every other.
—JOHN OWEN.

No place can be so pleasant but sin will lay it waste.
—JOHN TRAPP.

26 APRIL

SOCIETY

I dwell among mine own people.—2 Kings 4:13.
The company of his disciples.—Luke 6:17.
To keep company.—1 Cor. 5:11.

MAN is a creature in love with company.
—GEORGE SWINNOCK.

Many, although they cannot live asunder, yet they cannot live together.—HENRY SMITH.

For a commonwealth to want a chief, is the chief of all wants.
—THOMAS FULLER.

Some men, like Mercury, the good-fellow planet, are according to their company.—GEORGE SWINNOCK.

He that hath rich friends must not look upon himself as poor.
—JAMES JANEWAY.

Every variation from unity, is but a progression towards nullity.

It is ill being an inhabitant in any place where God is an exile.
—GEORGE SWINNOCK.

27 April

ATHEISM

The fool hath said in his heart, There is no God.—Psa. 14:1.
All his thoughts are, There is no God.—Psa. 10:4. (R.V.)

THOUGH there be many atheists in practice, yet there be no atheists in principle.—GEORGE SWINNOCK.

Every atheist is a grand fool.—STEPHEN CHARNOCK.

The devil himself, though he be no atheist, yet he doth all he can to make men atheists.—JOHN TRAPP.

Men may have atheistical hearts without atheistical heads.
—STEPHEN CHARNOCK.

Atheism is the main disease of the soul.—THOMAS ADAMS.

As beggars have learned to cant,* so atheists to pray.
—JOHN TRAPP.

If there be not a God, it is impossible there can be one.
—STEPHEN CHARNOCK.

---

* To cant = to sing (for pennies or food).

28 April

LITTLE THINGS

The little foxes, that spoil the vineyards.—Song of Sol. 2:15. (R.V.)
The day of small things.—Zech. 4:10.

A LITTLE boat may land a man at a large continent.
—GEORGE SWINNOCK.

The tallest oak was once an acorn.—THOMAS BROOKS.

The serpent of heart-apostasy is best killed in the egg of a small remission.—JOHN FLAVEL.

A small lackey may call us to a costly banquet.
—GEORGE SWINNOCK.

The pin in the temple serves for use as well the pinnacle.
—JOHN BOYS.

Small beginnings usher large proceedings.—WILLIAM JENKYN.

There must be an unit at least before any multiplication.
—THOMAS FULLER.

The flies and lice of Egypt were little creatures, but great plagues.
—GEORGE SWINNOCK.

29 April

WISDOM, KNOWLEDGE, AND SIMPLICITY

Give me now wisdom and knowledge.—2 Chron. 1:10.
I would have you ... simple concerning evil.—Rom. 16:19.

KNOWLEDGE searcheth the nature of a thing, and wisdom employs that thing to its proper use.

—STEPHEN CHARNOCK.

Knowledge without wisdom is like mettle in a blind horse.

—THOMAS BROOKS.

Knowledge is the foundation of wisdom.

—STEPHEN CHARNOCK.

Christ will have a serpent and a dove coupled together – wisdom and simplicity; and he bids, what God hath joined, that man should not sever.—RICHARD CLERKE.

Wisdom is the flower of knowledge, and knowledge is the root of wisdom.—STEPHEN CHARNOCK.

The serpent's eye (as one saith) does well only in the dove's head.—WILLIAM GURNALL.

30 April

ORDINANCES

Ordinances of divine service.—Heb. 9:1.

THE ordinances of God are the marts and fairs whereat Christians must trade for grace.—GEORGE SWINNOCK.

The body of a man can as soon labour incessantly without food, as the soul of a Christian can live continuously without ordinances.—WILLIAM SECKER.

The manna of the Spirit doth usually fall down in the dews of ordinances.—GEORGE SWINNOCK.

A man may go to hell with baptismal water upon his face.
—JOHN TRAPP.

The ordinances of God are the golden pipes through which he conveyeth the oil of grace from Christ, the olive tree.
—GEORGE SWINNOCK.

That man must famish at last who always feeds upon the dish instead of the meat.—WILLIAM SECKER.

To live above ordinances is to live below a saint.
—GEORGE SWINNOCK.

1 May

CHANGE

Bring forth the old because of the new.—Lev. 26:10
Meddle not with them that are given to change.—Prov. 24:21.

NETTLES have often been heirs to stately palaces.
—STEPHEN CHARNOCK.

There be many Labans; hot at first, cold at last; friendly in the beginning, froward in the end.—JOHN TRAPP.

Posting* passengers cannot be serious observers of any place.
—JEAN DAILLÉ.

We change purposes oftener than fashions.

—STEPHEN CHARNOCK.

Nature is relieved with changes, but clogged with continuance.
—THOMAS MANTON.

As it is not always fair weather with us in this life, so not always foul.—JOHN BOYS.

Many things fall out betwixt the chin and the chalice.

—JOHN TRAPP.

---

* Posting passengers = travellers in a hurry to complete their journeys, who make only brief stops at staging posts for refreshment.

2 May

BUSYBODIES

Some ... that work not at all, but are busybodies.
—2 Thess. 3:11.(R.V.)

A meddler in other men's matters.—1 Pet. 4:15. (R.V.)

We must not be busy bishops in other men's dioceses.
—JOHN BOYS.

Some have much science, little conscience.—THOMAS ADAMS.

It were better to be unknown than noted for misbehaviour.
—JOSEPH HALL.

An envious heart and a plotting head are inseparable companions.—THOMAS BROOKS.

Idleness is a kind of business.—JOHN TRAPP.

The curious and over-active spirit is unprofitable, for he will have one foot in the church, another in the court, and if God had made him a tripos,* he would have had a third in the camp.—JOHN BOYS.

Idle spirits will be ranging.—STEPHEN CHARNOCK.

---

* Tripos = a three-legged stool.

3 May

SIN AND JUDGMENT

*I will punish the world for their evil,
and the wicked for their iniquity.*—Isa. 13:11.
The wages of sin is death.—Rom. 6:23.

SIN and punishment go linked together with chains of adamant.—JOHN TRAPP.

Sin is no shrouder but a stripper.—HENRY SMITH.

Sin doth as naturally draw judgment to it as the loadstone doth iron.—JOHN TRAPP.

The farther from sin the more distant from danger.
—WILLIAM JENKYN.

Pollution is the forerunner of perdition.—JOHN TRAPP.

What is greatest in the rank of sins deserves the greatest misery in the rank of penalties.—STEPHEN CHARNOCK.

The face of the old world was grown so foul that God was fain to wash it with a flood.—JOHN TRAPP.

Take heed an hour produce not that which may shame us for ever.—GEORGE HUTCHESON.

4 May

FASTING, AND FEASTING

I wept and chastened my soul with fasting.—Psa. 69:10.
Ye ... eat the lambs out of the flock ... drink wine in bowls ... but they are not grieved for the affliction of Joseph.—Amos 6:3, 4, 6.

FEASTING days are soul-starving days, and fasting days are soul-fatting days.—WILLIAM JENKYN.

It is over-much feasting of Dives which of necessity maketh the fasting of Lazarus.—THOMAS FULLER.

Gluttony is the sepulchre of the living, and a kind of spiritual drowning of a man.—WILLIAM JENKYN.

Fasting which tames the body, without humility, makes proud the mind.—JOHN BOYS.

Surfeiting is the bird-lime of the soul's wings.
—WILLIAM JENKYN.

Dives fared deliciously every day; there was no Friday in his week, nor fasting in his almanac, nor Lent in his year.
—THOMAS FULLER.

5 May

SERVICE

Your reasonable service.—Rom. 12:1.
His servants ye are to whom ye obey.—Rom. 6:16.

CHRIST keeps no servants only to wear a livery.
—WILLIAM JENKYN.

God hath many servants, but little service in the world.
—THOMAS ADAMS.

An idle servant is in God's esteem an evil servant.
—GEORGE SWINNOCK.

They who will not wear Christ's yoke will much less bear his burden.—WILLIAM GURNALL.

No true Christian is his own man.—JOHN CALVIN.

It is an unanswerable dilemma: If the service of Christ were bad, why did you enter into it? If good, why did you depart from it?—WILLIAM JENKYN.

He serveth his greatest enemy who serveth the devil; his fellow, who serveth the lust of his flesh; his servant, who serveth the world.—JOHN BOYS.

6 May

THE MISER

I have made gold my hope.—Job 31:24.
Thou fool.—Luke 12:20.

A HARVEST may as well be looked for in a hedge as true grace in a gold-thirsty heart.—JOHN TRAPP.

The miser deprives himself of this world and God will deprive him of the next.—THOMAS ADAMS.

They are fools that fear to lose their wealth by giving, but fear not to lose themselves by keeping it.—JOHN TRAPP.

A poor man doth want many things, a rich miser wants everything.—JOHN BOYS.

It may well be said of money-lenders, they have no quicksilver, no current money.—JOHN TRAPP.

The miser and the rioter are opposites.—THOMAS ADAMS.

Many are, the richer the harder.—JOHN TRAPP.

7 May

FITNESS

That which is befitting.—Philem. 8. (R.V.)
By the hand of a fit man.—Lev. 16:21.
It was meet.—Luke 15:32.

A WOODEN key that opens the door is better than a golden one that cannot.—WILLIAM JENKYN.

What wise man would fish for gudgeons with golden hooks?
—THOMAS WATSON.

A garment which fits us is better for us, though it be plain, than one which is gaudy and three or four handfuls too big.
—WILLIAM JENKYN.

A hammer for the smith, a Homer for the school.—JOHN BOYS.

He [God] expects not a chapman* to truck with him, but an humble suppliant to be suitor to him.—WILLIAM GURNALL.

It is not fit we should deny God the cream and flower, and give him the slotten† parts and the stalks.—STEPHEN CHARNOCK.

Heavenly manna must be laid up in a golden pot.
—WILLIAM SECKER.

---

* Chapman = customer.
† Slotten = hollow, empty, worthless.

8 May

ATONEMENT

Our Lord Jesus Christ, by whom we have now received the atonement.—Rom. 5:11.

We were reconciled to God through the death of his Son. —Rom. 5:10. (R.V.)

THE blood of Christ is the seal of the testament.
—HENRY SMITH.

His being slain from the foundation of the world was the foundation of the world's standing.—ELISHA COLES.

In the creation the Lord made man like himself; but in the redemption he made himself like man.—JOHN BOYS.

The enmity between God and us began on our part; the peace which he hath made begins and ends with himself.

—JOHN OWEN.

The wrong that man had done to the divine majesty *should* be expiated by none but man, and *could* be by none but God.—JOHN HOWE.

Foregoing sins cannot be expiated by subsequent duties. Paying of new debts doth not quit the old score.

—THOMAS MANTON.

9 May

SATAN, THE PRINCE OF THIS WORLD

The prince of this world.—John 12:31.
The god of this world.—2 Cor. 4:4.

SATAN'S diocese, that odd dirty corner of the universe.
—THOMAS MANTON.

Satan is a king given in God's wrath.—WILLIAM GURNALL.

The devil is a busy bishop in his diocese.—THOMAS WATSON.

We are sure of his [the devil's] company, though uncertain how we came by it.—THOMAS WATSON.

The devil's circuit is greater than the Pope's.—HENRY SMITH.

Satan paints God with his own colours.—STEPHEN CHARNOCK.

The devil shall never lift his head higher than the saint's heel.
—WILLIAM GURNALL.

Better starve than go to the devil for provender.
—THOMAS WATSON.

10 May

FAITH ESSENTIAL

Without faith it is impossible to please him.—Heb. 11:6.
Even the plowing [lamp, R.V.] of the wicked, is sin.—Prov. 21:4.

A SPLENDID action without faith is but moral; whereas one of a less glittering is spiritual with it.
—STEPHEN CHARNOCK.

Till men have faith in Christ, their best services are but glorious sins.—THOMAS BROOKS.

It is a sad sign that our ways please not God, when his ways please not us at all.—JOHN OWEN.

Moral virtue may wash the outside, but faith washes the inside.
—THOMAS ADAMS.

Neither is faith without a godly life, neither can a godly life proceed but from faith.—JOHN CALVIN.

Without faith the devil can show as good a coat of arms as we can.—THOMAS WATSON.

Whatever your wants are, want not faith, and you cannot want supplies.—STEPHEN CHARNOCK.

11 May

THE GAIN OF DEATH AND THE FEAR OF DEATH

For to me ... to die is gain.—Phil. 1:21.
Fear of death.—Heb. 2:15.

THE wheels of death's chariot may rattle and make a noise, but they are to carry a believer to Christ.

—THOMAS WATSON.

The body's death to this world is the soul's birth into another world.—MATTHEW HENRY.

The worst of a saint is past when he dieth.

—GEORGE SWINNOCK.

The good man's *best*, and the bad man's *worst*, lie in *shall be's,* in reversion.—RALPH VENNING.

Let thy hope of heaven master thy fear of death.

—WILLIAM GURNALL.

Death breaks the union between the body and the soul but perfects the union between Christ and the soul.

—THOMAS WATSON.

Death is never sudden to a saint; no guest comes unawares to him who keeps a constant table.—GEORGE SWINNOCK.

12 May

VACILLATION

Be no more children, tossed to and fro, and carried about with every wind of doctrine.—Eph. 4:14.

THE unstable man is a live weathercock.—THOMAS ADAMS.

How many by the wind of popular breath have been blown to hell.—THOMAS WATSON.

God likes not qualmy Christians, good by fits.—JOHN TRAPP.

He that is *multivolus*, i.e., many-willed, will surely be *malevolus*, i.e., evil-willed.—THOMAS ADAMS.

As feathers will be blown every way, so will feathery Christians.
—THOMAS WATSON.

A hireling will be a changeling.—WILLIAM SECKER.

No seal can be set on running water.—THOMAS ADAMS.

A smooth, if a false way should not delight us; nor should a rugged, if a right way, dishearten us.—WILLIAM JENKYN.

13 May

REPUTATION

That men say not.—Judg. 9:54.
Them which were of reputation.—Gal. 2:2.

AMONG men reputation is measured by the acre.
—THOMAS ADAMS.

A man is better known by the features of his face than by the prints of his feet.—STEPHEN CHARNOCK.

A man's honest fame is like the merchant's wealth, got in many years and lost in an hour.—JOHN BOYS.

Wounds of reputation no physician can cure.
—THOMAS WATSON.

It is a great mercy when our names outlive us; it is a great punishment when we outlive our names.—WILLIAM JENKYN.

When a man is in favour with a prince, all the courtiers will be observant of him.—STEPHEN CHARNOCK.

Rose water is not the less sweet because one writes wormwood on the glass.—WILLIAM GURNALL.

14 May

MEEKNESS

The meek shall inherit the earth; and shall delight themselves in the abundance of peace.—Psa. 37:11.

A soft answer turneth away wrath.—Prov. 15:1.

'THE meek shall inherit the earth', and have heaven to boot.—JOHN TRAPP.

A meek man is a good neighbour.—GEORGE SWINNOCK.

You must see, and not see, if you will be of a meek spirit.
—JEREMIAH BURROUGHS.

The purest gold is the most pliable.—WILLIAM SECKER.

Hard to soft doth no hurt, as a bullet against a woolsack.
—JOHN TRAPP.

That which will break a passionate man's heart will not break a meek man's sleep.—THOMAS BROOKS.

Speech endeth anger, silence nourisheth it.—JOHN TRAPP.

It were good strife amongst Christians, one to labour to give no offence, and the other to labour to take none.
—RICHARD SIBBES.

15 May

APOSTATES

Demas hath forsaken me.—2 Tim. 4:10.
Them that are turned back from the Lord.—Zeph. 1:6.
They went out from us, but they were not of us.—1 John 2:19.

NONE can be termed apostates, but such as have previously made a profession of Christ.—JOHN CALVIN.

None sink so far into hell as those that come nearest heaven, because they fall from the greatest height.
—WILLIAM GURNALL.

It were far easier to write a book of apostates in this age than a book of martyrs.—JOHN TRAPP.

Every apostate is in the highway to become a persecutor.
—WILLIAM JENKYN.

The apostate drops as a windfall into the devil's mouth.
—THOMAS WATSON.

Apostates have martial law, they run away but into hell-mouth.
—JOHN TRAPP.

Judas arose from his Master's table, to sit at the devil's.
—WILLIAM GURNALL.

16 May

WORDS AND WISHES

They did chide with him sharply.—Judg. 8:1.
Pleasant words are as an honeycomb.—Prov. 16:24.
They ... wished for the day.—Acts 27:29.

WORDS are wind; ay, but they are that wind that blows up this fire [anger] to a mighty heat.
—JEREMIAH BURROUGHS.

Soft words do best with strong arguments. The iron of Naphtali's foot was dipped in oil.—JEAN DAILLÉ.

Five words cost Zachariah forty weeks' silence.
—THOMAS FULLER.

He is an ill wooer that wanteth words.—NEHEMIAH ROGERS.

He that will not speak idly must think what he speaks; and he that will not speak falsely must speak what he thinks.
—JOHN BOYS.

The belly is not filled with words, or the back clothed with wishes.—THOMAS MANTON.

A man cannot come to his journey's end with wishing.
—RICHARD SIBBES.

17 May

SATAN THE ADVERSARY

Your adversary the devil, as a roaring lion, walketh about, seeking whom he may devour.—1 Pet. 5:8.

THE devil, that great peripatetic.—JOHN TRAPP.

The devil pieceth the fox's skin of seducers with the lion's skin of persecutors.—WILLIAM GURNALL.

The devil hunts more as a fox than as a lion; his snares are worse than his darts.—THOMAS WATSON.

When Satan roars they have given him a full blow.
—WILLIAM JENKYN.

Satan watcheth for those vessels that sail without a convoy.
—GEORGE SWINNOCK.

It is not safe parleying with the devil.—JOHN TRAPP.

Satan is an archer who can shoot to a nicety.
—WILLIAM GURNALL.

He that sings syren-like now, will devour lion-like at last.
—JOHN DURANT.

18 May

MASTERS AND GOVERNORS

Them that are your masters.—Eph. 6:5.
Tutors and governors.—Gal. 4:2.

THE error of the master is the temptation of the scholar.
—WILLIAM JENKYN.

Where all govern there is no government.—THOMAS HALL.

Unless man were his own maker, he cannot have any title to become his own master.—WILLIAM GURNALL.

That man is not worthy to be served who cannot afford that his servant should serve God as well as himself.—HENRY SMITH.

They who most oppose government in others, most desire the government over others.—WILLIAM JENKYN.

Know by the servants what master dwells in a house.
—WILLIAM GURNALL.

A ruler that is a bribe-taker is a thief in robes.
—GEORGE SWINNOCK.

Government without governors is but a notion.
—WILLIAM JENKYN.

19 May

PARADOXES

We have seen strange things [lit. *paradoxes**] *to day.*—Luke 5:26.

SIN is never less quiet than when it seems to be most quiet.
—JOHN OWEN.

We cannot seek God till we have found him.
—GEORGE SWINNOCK.

Strange things agree in a Christian.—RICHARD SIBBES.

A man cannot have faith without asking, neither can he ask it without faith.—EDWARD MARBURY.

God is never more angry than when he is not angry.
—WILLIAM JENKYN.

Heaven must be in thee before thou canst be in heaven.
—GEORGE SWINNOCK.

While the pilot keeps his ship, his ship keeps him.
—THOMAS WATSON.

It is the greatest bondage in the world to have most freedom in ill.—RICHARD SIBBES.

---

* Only occurrence in the New Testament.

20 May

THE EYE

The light of the body is the eye: if therefore thine eye be single, thy whole body shall be full of light. But if thine eye be evil, thy whole body shall be full of darkness. If therefore the light that is in thee be darkness, how great is that darkness!—Matt. 6:22, 23.

UNCHASTE eyes are the heralds of an unchaste heart.
—JOHN CALVIN.

God hath made the same organ for seeing and weeping.
—GEORGE SWINNOCK.

The eye is the principal Cinque Port* of the soul.
—THOMAS FULLER.

If the eye be once inflamed, it will be hard to stand out long against sin.—JOHN BUNYAN.

There is affection as well as vision in the eye.—THOMAS TAYLOR.

Princes see by their servants' eyes more than by their own.
—STEPHEN CHARNOCK.

In love the eyes are the leader.—THOMAS ADAMS.

A pure eye only can see a pure God.—GEORGE SWINNOCK.

---

* Cinque Port = a reference to an ancient confederation of five English coastal ports in Kent and Sussex, originally formed for military and trade purposes (Hastings, New Romney, Hythe, Dover, and Sandwich).

21 May

SIN

This abominable thing that I hate.—Jer. 44:4.

SIN is the dare of God's justice, the rape of his mercy, the jeer of his patience, the slight of his power, and the contempt of his love.—JOHN BUNYAN.

The only dreadful thing is sin.—ELISHA COLES.

Sin is the strength of death and the death of strength.
—THOMAS ADAMS.

The greatest violation of conscience is the greatest of sins.
—JOHN FLAVEL.

Put sin into its best dress, it is but gilded damnation.
—WILLIAM JENKYN.

Sin is an ill inmate that will not out till the house fall on the head of it.—THOMAS BROOKS.

No sin against God can be little, because it is against the great God.—JOHN BUNYAN.

To see sin as sin is hell.—THOMAS GOODWIN.

22 May

BEDS AND GRAVES

They buried him in his own sepulchres ... and laid him in the bed.—2 Chron. 16:14.

THOSE who lie down on beds of ivory must lie down in beds of earth.—GEORGE SWINNOCK.

We are more sure to arise out of our graves than out of our beds.—THOMAS WATSON.

Toothache hath raised many from their beds, it hath sent few to their graves.—THOMAS FULLER.

The sick-bed is the passage to the grave.—GEORGE SWINNOCK.

He that carries passions to bed with him will find the devil creep between the sheets.—WILLIAM SECKER.

He who hath laid up his heart in heaven will comfortably think of laying down his head in the earth.—GEORGE SWINNOCK.

The sepulchres of ministers are not the graves of the ministry.—STEPHEN CHARNOCK.

23 May

TEMPERANCE AND RESTRAINT

Temperate in all things.—1 Cor. 9:25.
See then, that ye walk circumspectly.—Eph. 5:15.

THE temperate may die, the riotous cannot live.
—THOMAS ADAMS.

I had rather be a sober heathen than a drunken Christian.
—WILLIAM GURNALL.

Knowledge seeks virtue, temperance finds it.—THOMAS ADAMS.

You should starve lust when you feed nature.
—THOMAS MANTON.

As the body is the temple of the Holy Ghost, so is Christian temperance the keeper of that temple.—WILLIAM JENKYN.

It is good to leave something that we may take, for fear of taking that we should leave.—THOMAS ADAMS.

He is a rare Rechabite* that never drank but when he was thirsty.
—THOMAS ADAMS.

---

* Rechabite = a member of an Israelite family, descended from Rechab, who refused to drink wine (see Jer. 35).

24 May

HUMILITY

Before honour is humility.—Prov. 15:33.
All of you gird yourselves with humility.—1 Pet. 5:5. (R.V.)

HUMILITY is both a grace and a vessel to receive grace.
—JOHN TRAPP.

Humility is a necessary veil to all other graces.
—WILLIAM GURNALL.

If the work be good, though it be never so low, humility will put a hand to it.—THOMAS BROOKS.

It is one of the hardest matters under the sun to become nothing in ourselves.—ELISHA COLES.

Moses had more glory by his veil than by his face.
—JOHN TRAPP.

Where humility is the corner-stone, there glory will be the top-stone.—WILLIAM SECKER.

Humility is the knees of the soul.—THOMAS ADAMS.

25 May

PARDON

I have blotted out, as a thick cloud, thy transgressions, and, as a cloud, thy sins.—Isa. 44:22.

GOD blots out not only the cloud but the thick cloud, enormities as well as infirmities.—THOMAS WATSON.

Sins are so remitted as if they never had been committed.
—THOMAS ADAMS.

Forgiveness is a pure gospel truth that hath neither shadow, footstep, nor intimation elsewhere.—JOHN OWEN.

Forgiveness is a golden thread spun out of the bowels of free grace.—THOMAS WATSON.

The gospel refuses to pardon no sin for which the soul can be humbled.—THOMAS ADAMS.

Pope's pardons are insignificant, like blanks in a lottery.
—THOMAS ADAMS.

26 May

DEATH UNIVERSAL

How doth the wise man die even as the fool!—Eccles. 2:16. (R.V.)
The common death of all men.—Num. 16:29.

THE statute of death is above the prerogative royal.
—THOMAS FULLER.

Death is that mistress of the world that will not be courted nor yet cast off by any.—JOHN TRAPP.

The oak outliveth the ash, and the ash the willow, yet all die.
—THOMAS GOODWIN.

We can see death in other men's brows, but not in our own bosoms.—JOHN TRAPP.

Against this arrest there is no bail.—GEORGE SWINNOCK.

Death takes not men in seniority, but sometimes sends them first to the burial that came last from the birth.
—THOMAS FULLER.

Death takes away difference between king and beggar, and tumbles both the knight and the pawn into one bag.
—THOMAS ADAMS.

27 May

TEMPORARY AND FALSE FAITH

These have no root, which for a while believe, and in time of temptation fall away.—Luke 8:13.

FAITH in temporary believers is as a guest comes for a night, and is gone.—THOMAS FULLER.

A temporary faith is like Jonah's gourd, which came up in a night and withered.—THOMAS WATSON.

Nothing can be more inconsistent with the nature of faith than a feeble, wavering assent.—JOHN CALVIN.

A presumptuous faith is an easy faith.—WILLIAM GURNALL.

He that maketh a bridge of his own shadow cannot but fall into the brook.—JOHN TRAPP.

A man trieth his horse which must bear him, and shall he not try his faith?—HENRY SMITH.

Faith is not an idle grace.—THOMAS MANTON.

28 May

PROVIDENCE

His kingdom ruleth over all.—Psa. 103:19.
The eyes of the Lord run to and fro throughout the whole earth.
—2 Chron. 16:9.

GOD made meat before mouths.—JOHN TRAPP.

Providence is crowned by the end of it.
—STEPHEN CHARNOCK.

God's works are never above right, though often above reason.
—THOMAS FULLER.

Providence is the perpetuity and continuance of creation.
—RICHARD SIBBES.

If Joseph had not been Egypt's prisoner, he had not been Egypt's governor.—WILLIAM SECKER.

God has more remote ends than short-sighted souls are able to espy.—STEPHEN CHARNOCK.

God's providence leaves room for the use of our prudence.
—MATTHEW HENRY.

Grace makes the promise, and providence the payment.
—JOHN FLAVEL.

29 May

MANY THINGS

I had many things to write.—3 John 13.

JEALOUSY never thinks itself strong enough.
—JOHN BUNYAN.

Perfection is the boundary of the strongest expectation.
—WILLIAM SECKER.

Opinion cannot err in matters of opinion.—THOMAS ADAMS.

The best drugs have their adulterates.—WILLIAM SECKER.

A long coat will soon be draggled.—THOMAS MANTON.

Sin never ruins but where it reigns.—WILLIAM SECKER.

The Lord's pleasure is the Lord's leisure.—THOMAS FULLER.

God looks most where man looks least.—WILLIAM SECKER.

Negative holiness requires no great pains.
—GEORGE SWINNOCK.

Sodom was burned, but the sins escaped.—HENRY SMITH.

30 May

UNTHANKFULNESS

Unthankful.—2 Tim. 3:2.
Where are the nine?—Luke 17:17.

MORE have gone away speeders than have gone away thankers.—HENRY SMITH.

It is ten-to-one that any leper returns to give praise to God.
—JOHN TRAPP.

Our unthankfulness is the cause of the earth's unfruitfulness.
—WILLIAM SECKER.

It is impossible we can be cruel to others, except we forget how kind Christ hath been to us.—JOHN FLAVEL.

Thankless men are like swine feeding on acorns, which, though they fall upon their heads, never make them look up to the tree from which they come.—JEAN DAILLÉ.

Unthankfulness is the devil's text.—JOHN BOYS.

A drop of praise is an unsuitable acknowledgment for an ocean of mercy.—WILLIAM SECKER.

There is no creature made worse by kindness, but man.
—JOHN FLAVEL.

31 May

CONTENTS AND MEANING OF SCRIPTURE

What saith the scripture?—Rom. 4:3.
Understandest thou what thou readest?—Acts 8:30.

WHERE the Scripture hath no tongue we must have no ears.—JOHN TRAPP.

I like those expositions that take the wings of a dove, and fly to the uttermost parts of the text.—EDWARD MARBURY.

The Scripture is the sun; the church is the clock.—JOSEPH HALL.

Paul's epistles are ours, though not in their inscriptions yet in their benefits.—WILLIAM JENKYN.

The Lord does not shine upon us, except when we take his word as our light.—JOHN CALVIN.

As a friend that is acquainted with his friend will get out the meaning of a letter or phrase which another could not that is a stranger, so it is in Scripture.—JOHN TRAPP.

1 June

OUTWARD AND INWARD

Ye tithe mint and rue and all manner of herbs, and pass over judgment and the love of God: these ought ye to have done, and not to leave the other undone.—Luke 11:42.

OUTWARD decency in the church is a harbinger to provide a lodging for inward devotion to follow after.
—THOMAS FULLER.

Outward expressions are but the badges and liveries of service, not the service itself.—STEPHEN CHARNOCK.

Outward ornaments make no inward alteration.
—WILLIAM JENKYN.

'Glorious within' and 'clothing of wrought gold' decipher the same person, and may not be separated.—ELISHA COLES.

It is safer eating with unwashed hands than unwashed hearts.
—HENRY SMITH.

God is not taken with the cabinet but the jewel.
—STEPHEN CHARNOCK.

Never content yourself with Elijah's mantle, without the Lord God of that mantle.—CHRISTOPHER NESSE.

2 JUNE

DESPAIR

Then Judas ... repented himself ... and departed, and went and hanged himself.—Matt. 27:3, 5.

JUDAS' despair was worse than his treason.
—THOMAS WATSON.

Reason says, the bigger the sinner, the less grounds of hope.
—JOHN BUNYAN.

Desperation is the ground of all sin.—RICHARD SIBBES.

Bankrupts care not to look into their books of accounts.
—JOHN FLAVEL.

The devil would make us wade so far in the waters of repentance, that we should get beyond our depth, and be drowned in the gulf of despair.—THOMAS WATSON.

Despair is Satan's masterpiece.—JOHN TRAPP.

Despair cuts the sinews of endeavour.—THOMAS WATSON.

3 JUNE

'IF…'

If I be.—2 Kings 1:10.
If thou wilt.—Judges 4:8.
If ye shall.—1 Kings 9:6.
If any man.—1 Sam. 2:16.
If there be.—1 Sam. 20:8.

IF thou wilt fly from God, the devil will lend thee both spurs and a horse.—THOMAS ADAMS.

If thou wouldst die comfortably, live conscientiously.
—GEORGE SWINNOCK.

If there were no God, consciences were useless.—JOHN CALVIN.

If I speak what is false, I must answer for it; if truth, it will answer for me.—THOMAS FULLER.

If the serpents were not in their kind wiser than we, we should not have been advised to be wiser than serpents.
—JOSEPH HALL.

If all things were done by chance, there could be no predictions.
—STEPHEN CHARNOCK.

If adultery walk in our streets, the plague will bear it company.
—THOMAS ADAMS.

4 JUNE

GOD—HIS BEING

Him that filleth all in all.—Eph. 1:23.
The same God which worketh all in all.—1 Cor. 12:6.

THERE can be but one Infinite.—ELISHA COLES.

God's centre is everywhere, his circumference nowhere.
—THOMAS WATSON.

God is neither shut up in, nor shut out of, any place.
—GEORGE SWINNOCK.

The word Father is personal, the word God essential.
—STEPHEN CHARNOCK.

God cannot look above himself, because he hath no superior.
—JOHN BOYS.

It is a great vacuity that he, who fills heaven and earth, cannot fill.—JOSEPH CHURCH.

The being of a God is the guard of the world.
—STEPHEN CHARNOCK.

He that fills all, must needs see and know all.—RICHARD SIBBES.

5 JUNE

FLATTERY

Neither at any time were we found using words of flattery.
—1 Thess. 2:5. (R.V.).

IF there were judges ordained for flattery, they would have no doings, there being so very few that will complain that they are flattered.—JOHN TRAPP.

Spiritual flatterers are commonly more respected than spiritual fathers.—WILLIAM JENKYN.

Flatterers are the worst of tame beasts.—THOMAS FULLER.

Let a flatterer be in your Paternoster, but not in your Creed; pray for him, but trust him no more than a thief.

—JOHN BOYS.

Depressing irons can smooth the greatest wrinkles in cloth, so can flattering tongues do as to the most deformed actions.
—THOMAS GOODWIN.

As long as there is a false heart there will be a fawning devil.
—RICHARD SIBBES.

Whilst an ass is stroked under the belly, you may lay on his back what burden you please.—THOMAS BROOKS.

6 June

MERE PROFESSORS

They profess that they know God; but in works they deny him.
—Titus 1:16.

He who is but a visible Christian, may, in a short time, cease to be so much as visible.—WILLIAM JENKYN.

If the lamp of profession would have served the turn, the foolish virgins had never been shut out.—JOSEPH ALLEINE.

The course of thy life will speak more for thee than the discourse of thy lips.—GEORGE SWINNOCK.

Profane professors are but wens* upon the face of religion, which God will one day cut off.—WILLIAM JENKYN.

Many will take the press-money,† and wear the livery of Christ, and yet never stand to their colours, nor follow their leader.
—JOSEPH ALLEINE.

To see a ship sink in the harbour of profession is more grievous than if it perished in the open sea of profaneness.
—WILLIAM SECKER.

There are many who are lip-servants but not life-servants.
—WILLIAM JENKYN.

---

* Wens = boils or other swellings or growths on the skin.
† Press-money = money paid to a man enlisted into the army.

7 June

MARRIAGE

If thou marry, thou hast not sinned; ... nevertheless such shall have trouble in the flesh.—1 Cor. 7:28.

MARRIAGE is both honourable and onerable.
—GEORGE SWINNOCK.

It is not evil to marry but good to be wary.—THOMAS GATAKER.

A feast! never more seasonable, surely, than at the recovery of the lost rib.—JOHN TRAPP.

First, he must choose his love, and then he must love his choice.
—HENRY SMITH.

He that grafts into a crab-stock is never likely to want verjuice.*
—GEORGE SWINNOCK.

As God by creation made two of one, so again by marriage he made one of two.—THOMAS ADAMS.

As it is said of Egypt, that as no country hath more venomous creatures, none more antidotes; so marriage hath many troubles, but withal many helps against trouble.

—JOHN TRAPP.

---

* Verjuice = a highly acidic juice made by pressing unripe grapes, crab-apples or other sour fruit.

8 June

WAR

The grievousness of war.—Isa. 21:15.
Changes and warfare are with me.—Job 10:17. (R.V.)
Beat your plowshares into swords.—Joel 3:10.

WAR is the slaughter-house of mankind, and the hell of this present world.—JOHN TRAPP.

War makes both less meat and fewer mouths.
—THOMAS FULLER.

The noise of wars drowns the voice of laws.—JOHN TRAPP.

War is pleasant to those who never tried it.—JOHN CALVIN.

In war none are permitted to err twice.—JOHN TRAPP.

Woes may come from peace, but they must come from war.
—THOMAS FULLER.

Sin, Satan, and war have all one name; evil is the best of them. The best of sin is deformity, of Satan enmity, of war misery.—JOHN TRAPP.

9 June

THE POWER OF TEMPTATION

A tree to be desired.—Gen. 3:6.

SATAN never sets a dish before men that they do not love.
—THOMAS WATSON.

It is easier for a weak seducer to carry souls away, than for a strong Christian to keep them back.—WILLIAM JENKYN.

Ourselves are the greatest snares to ourselves.
—RICHARD BAXTER.

The world put on her holy-day apparel, when she was presented by the devil to our Saviour.—THOMAS FULLER.

To want temptations is the greatest temptation of all.
—SAMUEL RUTHERFORD.

Satan hath only a persuading sleight, not an enforcing might.
—THOMAS BROOKS.

It is not safe being at Satan's mess,[*] though our spoon be never so long.—JOHN TRAPP.

Everyone loves that most *without him* which is most suitable to somewhat *within him*.—THOMAS HORTON.

---

[*] Mess = dining table.

10 June

RULES

Walk according this rule.—Gal. 6:16.

A RULE must be open, or else it is no rule.—RICHARD SIBBES.

A peculiar gift may not be made a general rule.
—HENRY SMITH.

Gospel duties are to be performed with a gospel temper.
—STEPHEN CHARNOCK.

We are not saved *for* believing but *by* believing.
—THOMAS TAYLOR.

The love of sin must be out, ere the love of God be shown.
—GEORGE SWINNOCK.

Peace is never bought too dear but by sin.
—JEREMIAH BURROUGHS.

That which is begun in self-confidence will end in shame.
—RICHARD SIBBES.

He that walks by rule walks most safely.—THOMAS BROOKS.

God hath set it down for an eternal rule, that vexation and sin shall be inseparable.—RICHARD SIBBES.

11 June

THE PRECIOUSNESS OF CHRIST

I count all things ... but dung, that I may win Christ.—Phil. 3:8.
Unto you therefore which believe he is precious.—1 Pet. 2:7.

THE pearl of price cannot be a dear bargain.—JOHN TRAPP.

Where Christ reveals himself there is satisfaction in the slenderest portion, and without Christ there is emptiness in the greatest fullness.—ALEXANDER GROSSE.

They lose nothing who gain Christ.—SAMUEL RUTHERFORD.

The excellencies of Christ are perfectly exclusive of all their opposites.—JOHN FLAVEL.

Grace is a ring of gold, and Christ is the sparkling diamond in that ring.—THOMAS BROOKS.

To forsake Christ for the world, is to leave a treasure for a trifle; ... eternity for a moment, reality for a shadow; all things for nothing.—WILLIAM JENKYN.

12 June

OMISSIONS

Ye ... have omitted the weightier matters of the law.—Matt. 23:23.

Sins of omission are aggravated by knowledge.
—THOMAS MANTON.

Some sins of omission are like great men, that never go without many followers.—GEORGE SWINNOCK.

Make it your business to avoid known omissions, and God will keep you from feared commissions.—SAMUEL ANNESLEY.

He that leaves a duty may soon be left to commit a crime.
—WILLIAM GURNALL.

Not doing good, fits the heart for doing evil.
—GEORGE SWINNOCK.

Never was any wound healed by a prepared but unapplied plaster.—JOHN FLAVEL.

What good to have the shadow, though of a mighty rock, when we sit in the open sun?—WILLIAM GURNALL.

13 JUNE

STRONG DRINK

Beware, I pray thee, and drink not wine nor strong drink.
—Judg. 13:4.

BACCHUS and Venus are near neighbours; only voluptuousness hath a house between them.—THOMAS ADAMS.

If Christ would set up a pulpit at the alehouse door, some would hear him oftener.—JOHN TRAPP.

Wine tempers the heart like wax for the devil's impression.
—THOMAS ADAMS.

Drunken porters keep open gates.—HENRY SMITH.

Judgment is often at the threshold, while drunkenness and surfeit are at the table.—THOMAS ADAMS.

Such as wake much in *taverns* and *alehouses*, will be sure to sleep much in the ordinances.—CHRISTOPHER NESSE.

That is no medicinal cup to the body, that is poisonous to the conscience.—THOMAS ADAMS.

14 June

DESIRE

They ... sought him with their whole desire.—2 Chron. 15:15.

THE nearer to heaven in hopes, the further from earth in desires.—WILLIAM GURNALL.

The watches of our desires go too fast, they must be set back according to the sun-dial of God's pleasure.
—THOMAS FULLER.

A child, if it have not strong desires, it will be stilled with an apple; but if the desires be strong, nothing will still it but the dug.*—RICHARD SIBBES.

It is not the real excellence of a thing itself, but its known excellence that excites desire.—RICHARD BAXTER.

Desire will be a continual spring to diligence.—JOHN FLAVEL.

Desire is smoke and zeal is flame.—THOMAS GOODWIN.

Strong desires are like David's worthies, never satisfied till they come to the water of life.—RICHARD SIBBES.

---

* The dug = the breast's nipple.

15 JUNE

THINGS SECRET AND THINGS REVEALED

The secret things belong unto the Lord our God: but those things which are revealed belong unto us and to our children for ever.
—Deut. 29:29.

WHATEVER God's purposes be (which are secret), I am sure his precepts are plain.—JOSEPH ALLEINE.

God frames his language to our dullness, not to his own state.
—STEPHEN CHARNOCK.

Thomas acknowledged the divinity he did not see, by the wounds he did see.—JOHN BOYS.

How should finite comprehend infinite? We shall apprehend him, but not comprehend him.—RICHARD SIBBES.

Proud men are ashamed of Christ's humiliation, and, therefore, they fly to God's incomprehensible divinity.—JOHN CALVIN.

Mysteries are plain when the Lord opens, and plainest things are mysteries when he shuts.—JOSEPH CARYL.

16 June

THE POWER OF GRACE

*I laboured more abundantly than they all: yet not I,
but the grace of God.*—1 Cor. 15:10.

Grow in grace.—2 Pet. 3:18.

GRACE hath dominion though lusts are mutinous and seditious during the infancy thereof.—JOHN FLAVEL.

Weak grace may *do* for God, but it must be *strong* grace that will *die* for God.—WILLIAM SECKER.

Let those who are admitted into the college of grace disdain any longer to go to the school of the ceremonial law, which truly may be called the school of *Tyrannus*.

—THOMAS FULLER.

True grace is operative and will not lie dormant.—JOHN TRAPP.

Grace is light and discovers itself.—THOMAS BROOKS.

We discern the growth of grace, as the growth of plants, which we perceive, rather to have grown, than to grow.

—JOHN FLAVEL.

17 JUNE

WORK

To every man his work.—Mark 13:34.

THAT worker which needeth the fewest helps is the most perfect worker.—CHRISTOPHER NESSE.

The end of feeding is to fall to our calling.—THOMAS FULLER.

The master's mind is often more toiled than the servant's body.
—ROBERT LEIGHTON.

Greatest boasters are the smallest workers.—WILLIAM SECKER.

It is a more worthy thing to abound in work than to abound in wealth.—GEORGE SWINNOCK.

The *labourer*, not the loiterer, is *worthy of his hire*.
—HENRY WILKINSON.

Though you cannot do what you ought, yet you ought to do what you can.—CHRISTOPHER NESSE.

18 June

ASSURANCE KEPT OR LOST

Shew the same diligence to the full assurance of hope.—Heb. 6:11.
The full assurance of understanding.—Col. 2:2.

ASSURANCE hath a narrow throat and may be choked with a small sin.—THOMAS FULLER.

Confidence of salvation doth not contradict wariness of conversation.—THOMAS ADAMS.

The jewel of assurance is best kept in the cabinet of a humble heart.—THOMAS WATSON.

Like a leaky ship with a rich lading, the fear of sinking before she gets the port, takes away the owner's joy.
—WILLIAM GURNALL.

Fear to fall and assurance to stand are two sisters.
—THOMAS FULLER.

A well-grounded assurance is always attended by three fair handmaids: love, humility, and holy joy.—THOMAS BROOKS.

Assurance to persevere is a spark of heavenly fire, fed with the daily tinder of fear to offend God.—THOMAS FULLER.

19 JUNE

RUMOUR

Rumour shall be upon rumour.—Ezek. 7:26.

REPORTS relish of their relators.—THOMAS FULLER.

The first tale is good till the second be heard.
—JOHN TRAPP.

One eye-witness is better than ten ear-witnesses.
—THOMAS ADAMS.

An ill report is soon raised, but not so soon laid.
—GEORGE SWINNOCK.

Evil news rides post, while good news baits.*—JOHN MILTON.

Fame often creates something of nothing.—THOMAS FULLER.

Rumour is a loud liar, like a snowball that gathereth as it goeth.
—JOHN TRAPP.

---

* Rides post = rides uninterrupted between stage posts; baits = stops for refreshments.

20 June

PREVAILING PRAYER

I will not let thee go, except thou bless me.—Gen. 32:26.

GOD wrestled with Jacob with desire to be conquered.
—THOMAS FULLER.

Continued importunity is undeniable oratory.
—GEORGE SWINNOCK.

God can pick sense out of a confused prayer.—RICHARD SIBBES.

It was a sweet saying of one, 'O Lord, I have come to thee; but by thee, I will, never go from thee, without thee.'
—THOMAS BROOKS.

Breath is the first effort of life.—GEORGE SWINNOCK.

Bernard never went from God without God.—JOHN TRAPP.

All the prayers in the Scripture you will find to be reasoning with God, not a multitude of words heaped together.
—STEPHEN CHARNOCK.

21 June

DEATH OF CHRIST AND SIN

Our old man was crucified with him, that the body of sin might be done away.—Rom. 6:6. (R.V.)

IF Christ had not died, sin had never died in any sinner unto eternity.—JOHN OWEN.

Sin could not die, unless Christ died; Christ could not die, without being made sin; nor could he die, but sin must die with him.—ELISHA COLES.

All are not saved by Christ's death, but all which are saved, are saved by Christ's death.—HENRY SMITH.

Aqua fortis* is laid on letters of ink to eat them out, and so is the blood of Christ laid on the handwriting that is against us.—THOMAS GOODWIN.

The physician did die that the patient might live.—JOHN BOYS.

The wound of sin is not so broad as the plaster of Christ's blood.—THOMAS WATSON.

The first Adam runs away from God's presence; the second Adam runs after him to seek and recall him.

—THOMAS TAYLOR.

---

* *Aqua fortis* = lit. 'strong water', i.e. nitric acid.

22 June

FOOLS AND FOLLY

The foolishness of fools is folly.—Prov. 14:24.
Fools make a mock at sin.—Prov. 14:9.

HONOUR is as fit for a fool as a gold ring for a swine's snout.—JOHN TRAPP.

A fool hath always a knave attending on him.
—THOMAS GRANGER.

Fools are ever futuring.—WILLIAM JENKYN.

Evil is Hebrew for a fool.—JOHN TRAPP.

What wisdom itself counts foolishness, is folly to purpose.
—THOMAS FULLER.

Caligula, that threatened the air, if it durst rain when he was at his pastimes, durst not himself so much as look into the air when it thundered.—WILLIAM GURNALL.

Every natural man is a fool.—THOMAS GRANGER.

23 JUNE

PREACHING AND HEARING

Go thou near, and hear all that the Lord our God shall say: and speak thou unto us all that the Lord our God shall speak unto thee; and we will hear it, and do it.—Deut. 5:27.

A FAITHFUL minister must see before he say.
—EDWARD MARBURY.

As long as the messenger is loved, the message is not like to be loathed.—WILLIAM JENKYN.

His doctrine is best accepted whose person is most honoured.
—JOHN BOYS.

A minister without boldness is like a smooth file.
—WILLIAM GURNALL.

There is a form of doctrine delivered to us, and there is a form of words; we must not only say *this*, but *thus* saith the Lord.
—EDWARD MARBURY.

The hearer's life is the preacher's best commendation.
—THOMAS MANTON.

The Christian's life should put his minister's sermon in print.
—WILLIAM GURNALL.

24 June

THE SOVEREIGNTY OF GOD

The Lord did not set his love upon you, nor choose you, because ye were more in number than any people; ... but because the Lord loved you.—Deut. 7:7, 8.

GOD'S foreknowledge of what he will do doth not necessitate him to do.—STEPHEN CHARNOCK.

God is the cause of causes.—CHRISTOPHER NESSE.

As God did not at first choose you because you were high, so he will not forsake you because you are low.—JOHN FLAVEL.

Never look on the great attribute of sovereignty without your Mediator.—ELISHA COLES.

Salvation is no termer;* grace ties not itself to times.
—RICHARD CLERKE.

To be God and sovereign are inseparable.
—STEPHEN CHARNOCK.

We may not *reprehend* what we cannot *comprehend*.
—CHRISTOPHER NESSE.

In the wounds of Christ alone is predestination found and understood.—MARTIN LUTHER.

---

* Termer = one who came to town in term time.

25 JUNE

CHRIST AND THE CHURCH

Upon thy right hand did stand the queen in gold of Ophir. The king's daughter is all glorious within.—Psa. 45:9, 13.

CHRIST is the king of his church, and the church is the greatest queen in the world.—RICHARD SIBBES.

The king's daughter-elect, to make her a suitable match for his son, must be 'all-glorious within'.—ELISHA COLES.

The church comes out of Christ's side in the sleep of his death.
—WILLIAM JENKYN.

The excellence of the church does not consist in multitude but in purity.—JOHN CALVIN.

If the church be holy, be holy if you will be of the church.
—RICHARD BAXTER.

The church is taken out of dying Jesus' side, as Eve out of sleeping Adam's.—WILLIAM GURNALL.

It is between Christ and his church, as between two lute-strings – no sooner is one struck but the other trembles.
—THOMAS BROOKS.

26 June

POSSIBILITIES AND IMPOSSIBILITIES

With men this is impossible; but with God all things are possible.
—Matt. 19:26.

ALL things (but lying, dying, and denying himself) are possible to God.—CHRISTOPHER NESSE.

He that is not cannot be the cause that he is.
—STEPHEN CHARNOCK.

Sin must die or thy soul cannot live.—GEORGE SWINNOCK.

A man may hide God from himself, and yet he cannot hide himself from God.—WILLIAM SECKER.

As no place can be without God, so no place can compass and contain him.—STEPHEN CHARNOCK.

Sinners may oppose God's ways, but not his wrath.
—THOMAS WATSON.

Man can ruin but not renew himself.—GEORGE SWINNOCK.

They cannot escape God's iron rod who refuse to subject themselves to his golden sceptre.—STEPHEN CHARNOCK.

27 June

GROWTH IN SIN

Walketh ... in the counsel of the ungodly ... standeth in the way of sinners ... sitteth in the seat of the scornful.—Psa. 1:1.

MANY have yielded to go a mile with Satan that never intended to go two; but when once on the way have been allured further.—WILLIAM GURNALL.

First men break the tenth commandment by coveting, and then the eighth commandment by stealing.—THOMAS WATSON.

To begin a sin is to lay the foundation for a continuance; this continuance is the mother of custom, and impudence at last the issue.—JOHN BUNYAN.

First we practise sin, then defend it, then boast of it.
—THOMAS MANTON.

One sin is a step to another more heinous.—DAVID DICKSON.

A young sinner will be an old devil.—WILLIAM GURNALL.

Some think themselves improved in piety because they have left prodigality and reel into covetousness.—THOMAS FULLER.

28 June

WISE SPEECH

Sound speech, that cannot be condemned.—Titus 2:8.
The heart of the wise instructeth his mouth.—Prov. 16:23. (R.V.)

WHEN the heart is full of God … few words run then at the waste-spout.—JOHN FLAVEL.

A wise man will let down the bucket of his tongue into the well of his reason before he pour forth words.
—WILLIAM JENKYN.

He that weighs his words before he utters them shall prevent an after-reckoning for them.—JOHN TRAPP.

First be a seer and then a speaker.—EDWARD MARBURY.

It is impossible that a disordered heart should ever produce a well-ordered conversation.—JOHN FLAVEL.

It is as impossible for a shaking hand to write a straight line, as an unfixed judgment to have an even conversation.
—WILLIAM GURNALL.

29 JUNE

THE SPIRIT, THE WORD, AND THE NEW BIRTH

Born of water and of the Spirit.—John 3:5.
The washing of water by the word.—Eph. 5:26.
Born again ... by the word of God.—1 Pet. 1:23.

THE Spirit of God rides most triumphantly in his own chariot.—THOMAS MANTON.

The Christian is bred by the word, and he must be fed by it.
—WILLIAM GURNALL.

The word is the chariot of the Spirit, the Spirit the guider of the word.—STEPHEN CHARNOCK.

The word generates faith and regenerates us.—JOSEPH ALLEINE.

There are no still-born children in the family of grace.
—WILLIAM SECKER.

This word cannot beget without him, yet it is by this word that he begets.—ROBERT LEIGHTON.

The jewel of the word should not hang in our ears, but be locked up in a believing heart.—WILLIAM JENKYN.

30 June

WORLDLINGS

The children of this world.—Luke 16:8.

MEN have their name and denomination in the Scripture by that which they are ruled by.—RICHARD SIBBES.

The world is a tender mother to her children but a stepmother to strangers.—GEORGE SWINNOCK.

An owl's egg, though hatched by a dove or eagle, will prove but a night-bird.—ELISHA COLES.

The worldling's wisdom serves him (as the ostrich's wings) to make him outrun others upon earth, and in earthly things; but helps him never a whit toward heaven.—JOHN TRAPP.

He that loves the world is a worldling.—RICHARD SIBBES.

Those recusant guests in the gospel that pretended they therefore came not, because they had bought farms and oxen; but indeed it was because their farms and oxen had bought them.—JOHN TRAPP.

1 July

FEAR OF MAN

I feared the people, and obeyed their voice.—1 Sam. 15:24.
But the fearful.—Rev. 21:8.
Neither fear ye their fear, nor be afraid.—Isa. 8:12.

LET none but the servants of sin be the slave of fear.
—JOHN FLAVEL.

To conceal known adversaries is an argument of fear.
—THOMAS MANTON.

He is a fool, we say, that would be laughed out of his coat; but he is a double fool that would be laughed out of his skin, that would hazard his soul because loth to be laughed at.
—JOHN TRAPP.

Many lose heaven because they are ashamed to go in a fool's coat thither.—WILLIAM GURNALL.

The heart is not in case to receive promises till freed of false fears.—JOHN TRAPP.

God can secure us from fear, either by removing the thing feared, or by subduing the fear of the thing.
—WILLIAM BEVERIDGE.

2 July

CHRIST'S 'COME'

Come, ye blessed of my Father.—Matt. 25:34.
Let him that is athirst come.—Rev. 22:17.
I am the way ... no man cometh ... but by me.—John 14:6.

IF sinners have their 'Come' should not saints much more?
— JOHN TRAPP.

Whenever God blows with his wind, he looks that we should spread our sails.—TIMOTHY CRUSO.

Canst thou run the way without the Way?—JOHN KING.

Christ sends for us friendly, freely, frequently.
—THOMAS ADAMS.

The Way seeing his disciples out of the way, showed them the way.—JOHN BOYS.

God invites many with his golden sceptre whom he never bruises with his rod of iron.—THOMAS FULLER.

Nicodemus cometh haltingly to Christ, as a night-bird.
—JOHN TRAPP.

3 JULY

MEN AND WOMEN

Neither is the man, without the woman,
neither the woman without the man.—1 Cor. 11:11.

WHEN man lost free will, the woman found it, and still keeps it.—GEORGE SWINNOCK.

Woman takes her being from man, man takes his well-being from woman.—THOMAS ADAMS.

Women's wits are best at a pinch.—JOHN TRAPP.

When Adam was away, Eve was made a prey.—HENRY SMITH.

The weaker vessel may be a chosen vessel.
—CHRISTOPHER NESSE.

The weaker sex is the stronger in temptation.—THOMAS ADAMS.

Before man had any other calling, he was called to be a husband.
—HENRY SMITH.

4 JULY

ATTRIBUTES OF GOD

The excellencies of him.—1 Pet. 2:9. (R.V.)
His glorious attributes.—Eph. 1:12. (WEYMOUTH.)

THE holiness of God is his glory, as his grace is his riches.
—STEPHEN CHARNOCK.

One Almighty is more than all mighties.—WILLIAM GURNALL.

Glory is the sparkling of the Deity.—THOMAS WATSON.

Grace is the attribute God delights to honour.—ELISHA COLES.

The silver springs of grace and the golden springs of glory are in him.—THOMAS WATSON.

Clemency is one of the brightest diamonds in the crown of majesty.—WILLIAM SECKER.

The happiness of our souls depends upon God's other attributes, but the perpetuity of it upon his eternity.
—STEPHEN CHARNOCK.

He who is self-sufficient, all-sufficient, must needs be soul-sufficient.—WILLIAM JENKYN.

5 JULY

PEACE AND QUIETNESS OF SPIRIT

Surely I have stilled and quieted my soul; like a weaned child with his mother.—Psa. 131:2. (R.V.)

Attend upon the Lord without distraction.—1 Cor. 7:35.

YOU will find it as hard to get a composed spirit under great afflictions, as it is to fix quicksilver.—JOHN FLAVEL.

Inward peace is too precious a liquor poured into a filthy vessel.
—ROBERT LEIGHTON.

When the wind is still the great rain falleth.
—THOMAS MANTON.

Inward peace can only be espoused to *inward purity*.
—WILLIAM SECKER.

Peace is never bought too dear but by sin.
—JEREMIAH BURROUGHS.

Though the wind be laid and the storm over, thy heart must have some time to settle.—JOHN FLAVEL.

The quarter-day never comes amiss to him that hath always his rent ready.—GEORGE SWINNOCK.

6 July

THE DANGERS OF PROSPERITY

Hezekiah prospered in all his works. Howbeit ... God left him.
—2 Chron. 32:30, 31.

In prosperity the destroyer shall come.—Job 15:21.

AS hills, the higher the barrener; so men commonly the wealthier the worse; the more honour the less holiness.
—THOMAS FULLER.

Power is seldom a friend to humility.—WILLIAM GURNALL.

The heart of a Christian, like the moon, commonly suffers an eclipse when it is at the full, and that by the interposition of the earth.—JOHN FLAVEL.

Prosperity has its honey and also its sting; like the full of the moon, it makes many lunatic.—THOMAS WATSON.

What good is there in having a fine suit with the plague in it?
—JOHN TRAPP.

The getting of new wealth and honour makes some to lose their old eyes, so that they cannot see and discern their old kindred afterwards.—THOMAS FULLER.

7 JULY

UNBELIEF

An evil heart of unbelief.—Heb. 3:12.

WHEN God is not believed we must needs give credit to the devil.—STEPHEN CHARNOCK.

Unbelief, like Joab, strikes under the fifth rib, and kills outright.—GEORGE SWINNOCK.

Infidelity is always blind.—JOHN CALVIN.

It is common for men to make doubts when they have a mind to desert the truth.—SAMUEL RUTHERFORD.

Unbelief was the first sin, and pride was the first-born of it.
—STEPHEN CHARNOCK.

Unbelief was the crack in the glass, through which this inestimable water of life did leak out.—GEORGE SWINNOCK.

Unbelief is the shield of every sin.—WILLIAM JENKYN.

8 July

REASON AND FAITH

*They communed together and reasoned …
O fools, and slow of heart to believe.*—Luke 24:15, 25.

THE devil labours to put out the right eye of faith, and to leave us only the left eye of reason.—JOHN TRAPP.

Sense and reason are the crutches which weak faith leans on too much.—WILLIAM GURNALL.

Reason must neither be the rule to measure faith by, nor the judge thereof.—CHRISTOPHER NESSE.

Faith can rest in what it cannot comprehend.—JOHN OWEN.

Where reason cannot wade there faith may swim.
—THOMAS WATSON.

Abraham went, indeed, he knew not whither, but he did not go with he knew not who.—WILLIAM GURNALL.

What a short mete-wand[*] is natural reason to measure divine things by.—THOMAS TAYLOR.

---

[*] Mete-wand = measuring stick.

9 JULY

SABBATH

Six days shaft thou labour, and do all thy work: but the seventh day is the sabbath of the Lord thy God.—Exod. 20:9, 10.
The first day of the week ... the disciples were assembled.
—John 20:19.

THE Jews' seventh day was buried in Christ's grave.
—GEORGE SWINNOCK.

The translation of God's holy day ... from the Saturday to the Sunday, is not by patent in the Bible but only by pattern.
—JOHN BOYS.

A weekly Sabbath walls in our wild nature.
—CHRISTOPHER NESSE.

Better not do our own work any day, than not God's work on his day.—JOHN TRAPP.

On the week-days, every man riseth early to his trade; on the Lord's day, when the business of their souls is specially in hand, men usually sleep their fill.—THOMAS ADAMS.

The day of the Lord is likely to be a dreadful day to them that despise the Lord's day.—GEORGE SWINNOCK.

Make the Lord's day the market for thy soul.—JOHN BUNYAN.

10 July

READING AND WRITING

Give attendance to reading.—1 Tim. 4:13.
Having many things to write unto you.—2 John 12.

WRITING is an invention to deceive absence.
—WILLIAM JENKYN.

Reading maketh a full man, prayer a holy man, temptation an experienced man.—JOHN TRAPP.

The pen is an artificial tongue, the relief of the dumb and distant; by it the former speaks plain, and the latter aloud.
—WILLIAM JENKYN.

To read much and practise nothing is to hunt much and catch nothing.—THOMAS BROOKS.

The pen has the greatest auditories.—WILLIAM JENKYN.

In reading books, regard not so much the science* as the savour.—JOHN FLAVEL.

Satan hath prevailed more with his pen than his sword against the church.—WILLIAM JENKYN.

---

* Science = knowledge.

11 July

DESPISERS

Michal … saw king David leaping and dancing before the Lord; and she despised him in her heart.—2 Sam. 6:16.

And they said, Is not this Joseph's son?—Luke 4:22.

His bodily presence is weak, and his speech contemptible.
—2 Cor. 10:10.

REFUSE not gold from a dirty hand.—RICHARD SIBBES.

Despise no sanctuary and no auditory.—JOHN TRAPP.

Like foolish, frampole* children, we care not for the meat except we choose the spoon.—NEHEMIAH ROGERS.

It is far worse to despise a Saviour in his robes than to crucify him in his rags.—STEPHEN CHARNOCK.

God takes more unkindly the despising of his love than he doth the slighting of his wisdom.—THOMAS GOODWIN.

Despise not any man's meanness; you know not his destiny.
—JOHN TRAPP.

---

* Frampole = peevish.

12 July

FALSE FOLLOWING

Ye seek me ... because ye did eat of the loaves, and were filled.
—John 6:26.

WORLDLINGS in serving God, serve themselves of God; they follow him for loaves more than for love.
—JOHN TRAPP.

Follow not religion, as some hounds do the game, only for company.—WILLIAM JENKYN.

You may perish by false devotions as much as by real scandal.
—THOMAS WATSON.

There is not a more dangerous creature than a parasitical prophet.—JOHN TRAPP.

Truly that good was never worth seeking, that is not worth keeping.—WILLIAM SECKER.

Many follow God as Samson did his parents, till he light upon a honeycomb.—JOHN TRAPP.

Thou art never in the way of cure, till thou art sent out of thyself.—THOMAS TAYLOR.

13 JULY

DESPONDENCY

[Elijah] came and sat down under a juniper tree: and he requested for himself that he might die; ... I, even I only, am left.
—1 Kings 19:4, 10.

THEY have no need of our mocks, which I am afraid have too much of their own miseries.—THOMAS FULLER.

It is a scandal to religion to be over much dejected.
—RICHARD SIBBES.

O be not too quick to bury the church before she is dead.
—JOHN FLAVEL.

Despair acknowledgeth the truth in regard of the object, but doubteth in regard of the subject.—STEPHEN CHARNOCK.

He wanteth no other misery that is plagued with a fainting soul.
—JOHN KING.

When God would put a soul in tune for himself, he most commonly begins upon the lowest note.—JOHN BUNYAN.

The act may be perverted, though the faith cannot be subverted.
—JOHN FLAVEL.

14 July

LAWS, JUDGES, AND MAGISTRATES

Appoint magistrates and judges.—Ezra 7:25. (R.V.)
Ye shall hear the small as well as the great.—Deut. 1:17.

THAT city cannot be far from ruin, where the laws are not above the magistrate, but the magistrate above the laws.
—WILLIAM JENKYN.

Laws are better unmade than unkept.—HENRY SMITH.

An ignorant ruler is like a blind pilot.—THOMAS HALL.

A judge must have two kinds of salt in him; the salt of science to know the law, and the salt of conscience to determine according to the same.—JOHN BOYS.

Never did those magistrates long preserve their own names, who suffered God's to be profaned.—WILLIAM JENKYN.

A magistrate couchant* makes offenders rampant.
—THOMAS HALL.

---

* Couchant = lying down, sleeping, shutting his eyes.

15 July

RECOMPENSE

He had respect unto the recompense of the reward.—Heb. 11:26.

THEY that side with the saints shall thrive with the saints.
—JOHN TRAPP.

God is a better paymaster than the earth.—THOMAS ADAMS.

He that hath greatest layings out for God, shall have greatest comings in from God.—GEORGE SWINNOCK.

The nurse looks not for her wages from the child, but from the parent.—JOHN TRAPP.

God will not be served *for*, but he will not be served *without*, wages.—WILLIAM JENKYN.

Meditation of the reward is a good place for our souls to bait at,* but a bad place for our souls to lodge in.
—THOMAS FULLER.

Piety shall have riches without rust, wealth without want, store without sore, beauty without blemish, mirth without mixture.—JOHN TRAPP.

---

* Bait at = to stop for food and refreshment while on a journey.

16 July

GOD'S FAITHFULNESS

God himself hath said, I will never, never forsake you.
—Heb. 13:5. (WEYMOUTH.)

TWO negatives make an affirmative in grammar, but ten thousand will not make one in divinity.
—THOMAS GOODWIN.

If the end of one mercy were not the beginning of another, we were undone.—PHILIP HENRY.

Take notice not only of the mercies of God, but of God in the mercies.—RALPH VENNING.

God will preserve thee in thy ways not in thy wanderings.
—WILLIAM JENKYN.

Whatever God can do, he unquestionably will do, if he has promised it.—JOHN CALVIN.

As God numbers the hairs of his people, he must needs preserve their heads.—WILLIAM SECKER.

God doth not do many things that he can, but he doeth all things that he will.—GEORGE SWINNOCK.

17 July

THOUGHTS

The thoughts of thy heart.—Dan. 2:30.
The Lord knoweth the thoughts of man.—Psa. 94:11.

THOUGHTS are the most closeted acts of man.
—STEPHEN CHARNOCK.

Thy thoughts are vocal to God.—JOHN FLAVEL.

Esteem carries our thoughts.—RICHARD SIBBES.

Thoughts are the spies and messengers of the soul.
—THOMAS MANTON.

Thoughts are the immediate spawn of the original corruption.
—STEPHEN CHARNOCK.

Thoughts are the seeds of actions.—RICHARD SIBBES.

Thoughts are the purest offspring of the soul.
—THOMAS MANTON.

When thy fancy* is more mortified, thy thoughts will be more orderly and fixed.—JOHN FLAVEL.

---

* Fancy = imagination.

18 July

CAUSE AND EFFECT

The curse causeless shall not come.—Prov. 26:2.
Will a lion roar in the forest, when he hath no prey?—Amos 3:4.

WHERE the effect is good the cause is better, so where the effect is bad the cause is worse.—GEORGE SWINNOCK.

Anything that is imperfect cannot exist of itself.
—STEPHEN CHARNOCK.

A straw in the hand of a giant will make no deeper impression than if in the hand of a stripling.—ELISHA COLES.

It is the presence of the king that makes the court.
—RICHARD SIBBES.

The spider never builds but where there are flies.
—THOMAS ADAMS.

Fly the cause and thou fliest the effect.—GEORGE SWINNOCK.

Order being the effect cannot be the cause of itself.
—STEPHEN CHARNOCK.

A good stream hath a good spring.—RICHARD SIBBES.

19 July

THE WORLD

For all that is in the world, the lust of the flesh, the lust of the eyes, and the pride of life, is not of the Father, but is of the world.
—1 John 2:16.

The fashion of this world passeth away.—1 Cor. 7:31.

PLEASURE, profit, preferment are the worldling's trinity, to the which he performeth inward and outward worship.
—JOHN TRAPP.

There is no greater danger in the world than to live in the danger of the world.—THOMAS ADAMS.

It is dangerous dressing for another world by the looking-glass of this world.—WILLIAM SECKER.

Let us use the world, but enjoy the Lord.—THOMAS ADAMS.

The world may afford a felicity for our dust, the body, but not for the inhabitant in it.—STEPHEN CHARNOCK.

The world fashion is the worst fashion of all.—RICHARD SIBBES.

20 July

CHARITY

To do good and to communicate forget not.—Heb. 13:16.
Be rich in good works, ready to distribute, willing to communicate.
—1 Tim. 6:18.

BETTER lack all the rest than lack charity.—THOMAS ADAMS.

Charity offereth honey to a bee without wings.
—JOHN TRAPP.

Some men there be whose charitable deeds are as rare as an eclipse; these men deserve to be pardoned for their pious deeds, they are so seldom guilty of them.—THOMAS FULLER.

God's sons are known by their coat, that is, charity.
—THOMAS ADAMS.

Burn heretics with the fire of charity.—JOHN TRAPP.

A man that is charitable and not pure, is better to others than to himself.—THOMAS MANTON.

The river of charity springs from the fountain of piety.
—THOMAS ADAMS.

21 July

WRESTING SCRIPTURE

Things hard to be understood, which they that are unlearned and unstable wrest, as they do also the other scriptures, unto their own destruction.—2 Pet. 3:16.

THE word of life may be so distorted from the life of the word, till it becomes the food of death.—THOMAS ADAMS.

It is just (as one well said) that they who will not feed on the plain food of the word should be choked with the bones.
—JOSEPH ALLEINE.

Whom God intends to destroy, he gives them leave to play with Scripture.—MARTIN LUTHER.

They that will give God a new tongue shall feel his old hand.
—THOMAS ADAMS.

The word of God is adversary to none, but such as are their own greatest adversaries.—JOHN TRAPP.

How sad it is to carry these letters of heaven about us only as Uriah carried David's, for his own destruction.
—WILLIAM JENKYN.

Take the word from the Author not from the usurper.
—THOMAS ADAMS.

22 JULY

DILIGENCE

Be thou diligent. Prov. 27:23.
She gleaned in the field until even, and beat out that she had gleaned; and it was about an ephah of barley [over 50 lbs/22 kg weight].
—Ruth 2:17.

DILIGENCE may be a companion and comfort, where success is a stranger.—WILLIAM JENKYN.

One asking, what was the best compost to manure land, it was answered, The dust of the master's feet.—THOMAS FULLER.

Health cometh not from the clouds without seeking, nor wealth from the clods without digging.—JOHN KING.

It is better to be worn with using than with rusting.
—WILLIAM JENKYN.

Though sin brought in the husbandman's sweat, yet now, not to sweat would increase his sin.—JOHN FLAVEL.

The fen-man mends his banks in summer, lest his ground be drowned in winter.—THOMAS ADAMS.

The master's eye maketh a fat horse.—THOMAS FULLER.

23 July

PRAYER AND FAITH

The prayer of faith.—James 5:15.

FAITH baptizes prayer and gives it a name; it is called 'the prayer of faith'.—THOMAS WATSON.

Faith is to prayer what the feather is to the arrow.
—THOMAS WATSON.

When thou prayest, rather let thy heart be without words than thy words without a heart.—JOHN BUNYAN.

Patience in prayer is nothing but faith spun out.
—THOMAS WATSON.

As Joseph said, 'You shall not see my face unless you bring your brother Benjamin with you', so prayer cannot see God's face unless it brings its brother Faith with it.—THOMAS WATSON.

Prayer is the key of heaven, faith is the hand that turns it.
—THOMAS WATSON.

24 JULY

FREE GRACE AND FREE-WILL

Freely by his grace.—Rom. 3:24.
The will of man.—John 1:13.
How often would I ... and ye would not!—Matt. 23:37.

FREE-GRACE hath provided us a plank after shipwreck.
—THOMAS WATSON.

Abolish free-will and there is nothing to be saved; abolish free-grace and there is nothing wherewithal to save.—BERNARD

Free-grace will fix those whom free-will shook down into a gulf of misery.—THOMAS BOSTON.

If there were no will, there would be no hell.
—CHRISTOPHER NESSE.

Efficacious grace does not at all destroy natural liberty.
—THOMAS JACOMB.

The friends of free-will are the enemies of free-grace.
—JOHN TRAPP.

God could love nothing in Jacob above Esau but his own grace.—THOMAS MANTON.

25 JULY

AN EVIL HEART

Their heart was hardened.—Mark 6:52.
Their heart is divided.—Hos. 10:2.
The heart is deceitful.—Jer. 17:9.

SOME talk that the devil hath a cloven foot; but whatever the devil's foot be, to be sure his sons have a cloven heart.
—RICHARD ALLEINE.

No man perfectly knows his own heart; you think all well; this may not be assurance but secureness.—THOMAS ADAMS.

A vain heart out of prayer will be little better in prayer.
—WILLIAM GURNALL.

A stone in the heart is worse than in the kidneys.
—THOMAS WATSON.

Outward sins are sins of great infamy, but heart sins are sins of deeper guilt.—JOHN FLAVEL.

A hard knot must have an answerable wedge.—RICHARD SIBBES.

A little hope may melt that heart which despair would harden.
—GEORGE SWINNOCK.

26 July

REGENERATION

He saved us, by the washing of regeneration.—Titus 3:5.

REGENERATION is a spiritual change, conversion is a spiritual motion.—STEPHEN CHARNOCK.

Seeing we are born God's enemies, we must be new-born his sons.—RICHARD BAXTER.

Regeneration is, as it were, the minister which marrieth Christ and the soul together.—GEORGE SWINNOCK.

Adoption gives us the privilege of sons, regeneration the nature of sons.—STEPHEN CHARNOCK.

Repentance is a change of the mind, and regeneration is a change of the man.—THOMAS ADAMS.

Regeneration is the motion of God in the creature; conversion is the motion of the creature to God, by virtue of that first principle.—STEPHEN CHARNOCK.

As in generation, so in regeneration, we must be growing up to a full stature.—THOMAS ADAMS.

27 JULY

IGNORANCE

They willingly are ignorant.—2 Pet. 3:5.
Alienated from the life of God through the ignorance that is in them.—Eph. 4:18.

HE that knows nothing will believe anything.
—THOMAS FULLER.

Ignorance is the beaten path to hell.—WILLIAM JENKYN.

Ignorance is the mother of mischief.—THOMAS HALL.

It is a common fault, that ignorance is closely followed by obstinacy.—JOHN CALVIN.

Ignorance is not the mother of devotion but the grandmother of irreligion.—THOMAS ADAMS.

None but an ignoramus is an enemy to knowledge.
—HENRY WILKINSON.

An ignorant ruler is like a blind pilot.—THOMAS HALL.

An ignorant minister is none of God's making, for God gives gifts where he gives calling.—HENRY WILKINSON.

28 July

SPIRITUAL THINGS

Now concerning spiritualities.—1 Cor. 12:1. (lit.)
Comparing spiritual things with spiritual.—1 Cor. 2:13.

WE may as well judge of colours by moonlight, as of spiritual things by reason.—ELISHA COLES.

In spiritual things there is no envy.—RICHARD SIBBES.

Temporals are the bones; spirituals are the marrow.
—THOMAS BROOKS.

We cannot be spiritual priests till we be spiritual kings.
—STEPHEN CHARNOCK.

Spiritual things are against the stream, heaven is up the hill.
—RICHARD SIBBES.

Spiritual rest maketh no man idle, spiritual walking maketh no man weary.—NATHANIEL HARDY.

Our natural motions should be ordered for the God of nature, and spiritual ordered for the God of grace.
—STEPHEN CHARNOCK.

29 JULY

CONCEIT

Seest thou a man wise in his own conceit?
there is more hope of a fool than of him.—Prov. 26:12.

OF all fools the conceited fool is the worst.
—WILLIAM GURNALL.

He is two fools that is wise in his own eyes.—JOHN TRAPP.

He who does not account himself nothing will soon esteem Christ so.—JEAN DAILLÉ.

A conceited scholar is no good learner.—GEORGE SWINNOCK.

Self-opinion is the bane of all virtue.—EDWARD MARBURY.

You never knew a man full of self-confidence and self-abasement together.—WILLIAM GURNALL.

Ignorance and confidence are often twins.
—GEORGE SWINNOCK.

30 July

TRIED FAITH

The trial of your faith.—1 Pet. 1:7.
The trying of your faith worketh patience.—James 1:3

THE Christian must trust in a withdrawing God.
—WILLIAM GURNALL.

There is no place for faith, if we expect God to fulfil immediately what he promises.—JOHN CALVIN.

That poor woman of Canaan took up the bullets Christ shot at her, and with a humble boldness of faith sends them back again in her prayer.—WILLIAM GURNALL.

Faith should be above all that befalleth us.—THOMAS MANTON.

Faith may be shaken in, not out of the soul.—JEAN DAILLÉ.

Faith is safe when in danger, and in danger when secure.
—ROBERT LEIGHTON.

When Satan borrows sense to speak one thing, let faith borrow Scripture to speak the contrary.—DAVID DICKSON.

31 July

THE LAW AND THE GOSPEL

The glorious gospel of the blessed God.—1 Tim. 1:11.
The law of truth.—Mal. 2:6.

THE law gives menaces, the gospel gives promises.
—THOMAS ADAMS.

The law was for the old man to mortify him, and the gospel for the new man to comfort him.—HENRY SMITH.

The law is a gospel prefigured, and the gospel is a law consummated.—BISHOP HALL.

As a lively faith is the best gloss upon the gospel, so dutiful obedience is the best commentary upon the law.
—JOHN BOYS.

The law is a court of justice, but the gospel a throne of grace.
—GEORGE SWINNOCK.

The law by which God rules us, is as dear to him as the gospel by which he saves us.—WILLIAM SECKER.

The law is a hammer to break us, the gospel God's oil to cure us.
—STEPHEN CHARNOCK.

1 August

PROCRASTINATION

While he lingered, the men laid hold upon his hand.—Gen. 19:16.
When I have a convenient season, I will call for thee.—Acts 24:25.

IF God's *today* be too soon for thy repentance, thy *tomorrow* may be too late for his acceptance.—WILLIAM SECKER.

He that saith he will be good tomorrow, he saith he will be wicked today.—JAMES JANEWAY.

There be not many Lots, but many linger like Lot.
—HENRY SMITH.

Delay is a kind of denial.—TIMOTHY CRUSO.

Many think not of living any holier, till they can live no longer.
—WILLIAM SECKER.

Let us not have our oil to buy when we should have it to burn.
—THOMAS FULLER.

That which keeps us from living today, the thought of living tomorrow.—JAMES JANEWAY.

One Lot is enough in a family.

2 AUGUST

USURY

Thou shalt not give him thy money upon usury.—Lev. 25:37.

THE usurer loveth the borrower as the ivy loveth the oak.
—HENRY SMITH.

The usurer, like the ostrich, can digest any metal; but especially money.—JOHN TRAPP.

It were a blessed ship that could quite transport usury.
—THOMAS ADAMS.

Restitution is the repentance of usury.—HENRY SMITH.

Usurers may well be compared to the timber worm, which to touch is as soft as silk, but hath teeth so hard as that it eats the oak.—NEHEMIAH ROGERS.

I read of a woman whom Satan had bound (Luke 13:16) and truly he is almost in as bad a condition whom the usurer hath bound.—THOMAS WATSON.

If he be a fool that lays up his own goods, find out a name for him that extorts other men's.—THOMAS ADAMS.

Usurers make beggars, even as lawyers make quarrellers.
—HENRY SMITH.

3 AUGUST

GIVING AND RECEIVING REPROOF

Them that sin reprove in the sight of all.—1 Tim. 5:20. (R.V.)
He that regardeth reproof is prudent.—Prov. 15:5.

REPROOFS should be as oils or ointments, gently rubbed in by the warm fire of love.—GEORGE SWINNOCK.

An open reproof of our betters is little better than a libel.
—THOMAS FULLER.

Private reproof is the best grave to bury private faults in.
—GEORGE SWINNOCK.

If Noah be drunk, who shall reprove Ham?—HENRY SMITH.

Admonition is like physic,* rather profitable than pleasant.
—GEORGE SWINNOCK.

Next to the not deserving a reproof, is the well taking of it.
—JOHN TRAPP.

Reproof is an edged tool, and must not be jested with.
—GEORGE SWINNOCK.

It was well done of Paul to reprove Peter to his face, and it was well done of Peter to praise Paul in his absence.
—THOMAS ADAMS.

---

* Physic = medicine.

4 August

HYPOCRITES AFRAID OF PERSECUTION

In that day, ... the [false] prophets shall be ashamed every one of his vision.—Zech. 13:4.

GILDED potsherd may shine till it cometh to scouring.
—THOMAS MANTON.

When grapes come to the press they come to the proof.
—GEORGE SWINNOCK.

A rotten apple discovers itself in a windy day.
—WILLIAM JENKYN.

The Lord uses his flail of tribulation to separate the chaff from the wheat.—JOHN BUNYAN.

No hypocrite can bear the cross.—HENRY SMITH.

We must not spread our sails of profession in a calm, and furl them up when the wind riseth.—WILLIAM GURNALL.

A little chaff may abide in the floor if the wind does not blow.
—JEAN DAILLÉ.

Hereafter all paint must fall off which is not laid in the oil of sincerity.—WILLIAM JENKYN.

5 August

IDLENESS AND TEMPTATION

At the time when kings go forth to battle ... David tarried still at Jerusalem ... and walked upon the roof of the king's house: and from the roof he saw a woman washing herself.—2 Sam. 11:1, 2.

IDLENESS tempts the devil to tempt.—THOMAS WATSON.

An idle man is the devil's tennis ball, tossed by him at pleasure.—JOHN TRAPP.

Idleness is the very source of sin.—THOMAS BROOKS.

The sitting bird is the fowler's mark.—WILLIAM JENKYN.

The idle man may call the prodigal brother.
—GEORGE SWINNOCK.

He that wants employment never wants temptation.
—THOMAS WATSON.

While we work not ourselves, Satan works on us.
—WILLIAM JENKYN.

Let us deal with idleness and wantonness as Philip of Macedon did with two such persons, cause the one to drive the other out of our coasts.—THOMAS ADAMS.

6 August

GRACE AND GRACES

The grace of our God.—2 Thess. 1:12.
The praise of the glory of his grace.—Eph. 1:6.

GRACE is the freeness of love.—THOMAS GOODWIN.

True grace when weakest is stronger than false when strongest.—WILLIAM GURNALL.

Grace is of a noble offspring; it neither turns man into stocks* nor Stoics.—THOMAS BROOKS.

Grace is of that nature that it cannot possibly have any by-end.
—STEPHEN CHARNOCK.

Grace is not native but donative.—WILLIAM JENKYN.

Faith is the champion of grace, and love the nurse, but humility the beauty of grace.—THOMAS BROOKS.

There is a greater, gulf between grace and no grace than between weak grace and strong.—WILLIAM GURNALL.

---

* Stocks = anything fixed, solid or senseless; a stupid person.

7 August

BUSINESS AND SPIRITUAL THINGS

Martha, Martha, thou art careful and troubled about many things: but one thing is needful.—Luke 10:41, 42.

MORE business than thou canst well manage is like more meat than thou canst well digest, which will quickly make a sickly soul.—JOHN FLAVEL.

Stars which have least circuit are nearest the pole; and men who are least perplexed with business are commonly nearest to God.—THOMAS BROOKS.

He that will not spare time from his present business for his future blessedness is like to lose both.—GEORGE SWINNOCK.

That man who is a labouring bee for earthly prosperity will be but an idle drone for heavenly felicity.—WILLIAM SECKER.

Religion must be your business, all other things but your by-business.—CHRISTOPHER NESSE.

Religion never goes in more danger than when in a crowd of worldly business.—WILLIAM GURNALL.

8 August

THE FEAR OF GOD

So did not I, because of the fear of God.—Neh. 5:15.
The fear of the Lord is clean, enduring for ever.—Psa. 19:9.
Moved with godly fear.—Heb. 11:7. (R.V.)

HE who fears God can never find a place dark enough to offend.—WILLIAM JENKYN.

The fear of God is both a virtue and a keeper of other virtues.
—JOHN TRAPP.

As the embankment keeps out the water, so the fear of the Lord keeps out uncleanness.—THOMAS WATSON.

The best way never to fall is ever to fear.—WILLIAM JENKYN.

As the sunshine puts out the fire, so does the fear of God the fire of lust.—JOHN TRAPP.

The height of God must lay man low.—GEORGE SWINNOCK.

As faith is a grace that feeds all the rest, so fear is a grace that guards all the rest.—WILLIAM SECKER.

9 August

PRIDE'S RISE AND FALL

The pride of thine heart hath deceived thee, thou ... that saith in his heart, Who shall bring me down to the ground?—Obad. 3.

PRIDE loves to climb up, not as Zacchaeus to see Christ, but to be seen.—WILLIAM GURNALL.

A foolish king in a throne is an ape upon the house-top, highly perched, but absurdly conditioned.—JOHN KING.

Haman will never leave lifting up his head, till it be lifted a story higher than he would have had it.—THOMAS ADAMS.

The cackling hen loseth her egg; so doth the vain-glorious giver his reward.—JOHN TRAPP.

Vain glory is the worm that breeds in the best fruit of the wicked.—WILLIAM JENKYN.

As death is the last enemy, so pride the last sin that shall be destroyed in us.—JOHN BOYS.

10 August

SELF-EXAMINATION

Let a man examine himself.—1 Cor. 11:28.
Examine yourselves, whether ye be in the faith.—2 Cor. 13:5.

SELF-EXAMINATION is the beaten path to perfection.
—WILLIAM SECKER.

Self-examination is a spiritual inquisition set up in the soul.
—THOMAS WATSON.

Examination is the eye of the soul.—HENRY SMITH.

The reason why there is so little self-condemnation is because there is so little self-examination.—WILLIAM SECKER.

You must come to the knowledge of, before you can amend, yourself.—LANCELOT ANDREWS.

Contemplation is a perspective glass to see our Saviour in; but *examination* is a looking-glass to view ourselves in.
—WILLIAM SECKER.

See that thou show thyself the judge, not the patron of thy sins.—LANCELOT ANDREWS.

11 AUGUST

FALSE ZEAL

And he [Jehu] said, Come with me, and see my zeal for the Lord.
—2 Kings 10:16.

THE flame of Jehu's zeal was but kitchen fire.
—WILLIAM JENKYN.

It is weakness to be hot in a cold matter, but worse to be cold in a hot matter.—JOHN TRAPP.

Blazing comets soon evaporate.—THOMAS WATSON.

Feigned zeal is just like a waterman, that looks one way and rows another way; *pretends* one thing and *intends* another.
—GRIFFITH WILLIAMS.

Nothing violent is long permanent.—THOMAS FULLER.

Nebuchadnezzar destroyed idols that he might be worshipped.
—HENRY SMITH.

Hot at hand seldom holds out.—JOHN TRAPP.

Some have a true zeal for a false religion, and others have a false zeal of a true religion.—THOMAS ADAMS.

12 August

THE CHRISTIAN AND DEATH

*I am now ready to be offered,
and the time of my departure is at hand.*—2 Tim. 4:6.

A GODLY man is free from the sting, but not from the stroke, from the curse, but not from the cross of death.
—GEORGE SWINNOCK.

Death will cut us down, but he shall not eternally keep us down.
—WILLIAM SECKER.

To die well is a long art, but we have no long time to learn it.
—THOMAS ADAMS.

Death is only a grim porter to let us into a stately palace.
—RICHARD SIBBES.

To die is a business no man doth but once, and it is a business of the greatest moment of any we ever performed; and therefore to be directed and assisted in it, is answerably a great blessedness.—THOMAS GOODWIN.

Death, at the most, can get but a clay-pawn till your Lord take the King's keys and open your graves.
—SAMUEL RUTHERFORD.

13 AUGUST

PROMISES

Exceeding great and precious promises.—2 Pet. 1:4.

IT is better to be low as hell with a promise than in paradise without one.—JOHN FLAVEL.

Christ's performances outstrip his promises.
—NEHEMIAH ROGERS.

A great part of a Christian's estate lies in bonds and bills of God's hand.—JOHN TRAPP.

The very possession of the world is not half so sure as God's promises.—THOMAS ADAMS.

Grace and truth are the two ingredients of an evangelical promise.—JOHN OWEN.

Wherever the command of believing comes, it is always with a promise.—JAMES DURHAM.

The promises are good freehold, and yet little looked after.
—JOHN TRAPP.

Refused promises multiply woes.—DAVID DICKSON.

14 AUGUST

THE UNCERTAINTY OF RICHES

Riches certainly make themselves wings;
they fly away as an eagle toward heaven.—Prov. 23:5.
Riches are not for ever.—Prov. 27:24.

RICHES may leave us while we live, we must leave them when we die.—THOMAS FULLER.

Riches, as glass, are bright but brittle.—JOHN TRAPP.

That which was forty years in gathering, comes often to be spent in forty days revelling.—GEORGE SWINNOCK.

Riches are long in getting with much pains, hard in keeping with much care, quick in losing with more sorrow.
—THOMAS FULLER.

While riches are, they are not.—WILLIAM SECKER.

The world's golden sands are quicksands.—THOMAS WATSON.

Whom the sun-rising seeth in wealth, him the sun-setting may see in want.—THOMAS FULLER.

15 August

TRANSGRESSORS

The way of transgressors is hard.—Prov. 13:15.

BOTH authors, actors, and abettors of evil shall rue it together.—JOHN TRAPP.

Where iniquity breakfasts, calamity will be sure to dine; to sup where it dines and to lodge where it sups.—JOHN TRAPP.

Sin is the womb of our sorrows and the grave of our comforts.—THOMAS WATSON.

As every body hath its shadow, so hath every sin its fear.
—JOHN TRAPP.

Strayers are evermore sufferers for it.—JOHN FLAVEL.

Jews say there is no punishment befalleth them in which there is not still an ounce of that golden calf.—JOHN TRAPP.

Haman was exalted high, but not in safety.—JOSEPH CARYL.

16 AUGUST

WEAK CHRISTIANS

He [David] is weary and weak handed.—2 Sam. 17:2.
Many are weak and sickly among you, and many sleep.—1 Cor. 11:30.

ALL the king's subjects are not his champions.
—JOHN BUNYAN.

Weak Christians are very apt to three things: to choose their mercies, to choose their crosses, to choose their employments.—THOMAS BROOKS.

There is no place for any loose stone in God's edifice.
—JOSEPH HALL.

It was a charge long ago laid upon Christianity, that it was better known in leaves of books than in the lives of Christians.—WILLIAM GURNALL.

Such Christians as are like Pharaoh's lean kine,* reproach three at once: God, the gospel and their teachers.
—THOMAS BROOKS.

The weak Christian is willing to live and patient to die; but the strong, patient to live and willing to die.—JOHN BOYS.

---

* Kine = cattle.

17 August

GOD AS FRIEND OR ENEMY

There is a friend that sticketh closer than a brother.—Prov. 18:24.
He was turned to be their enemy.—Isa. 63:10.

GOD is as faithful in his menaces as in his promises.
—JOHN TRAPP.

He that hath God's heart cannot want* his grace.
—WILLIAM GURNALL.

God is the sweetest friend, but the worst enemy.
—THOMAS WATSON.

It is not safe to be at odds with the Ancient of Days.
—JOHN TRAPP.

God hath strength enough to give, but he hath no strength to deny.—WILLIAM GURNALL.

I had rather been in hell with God than in heaven without him, and it were far safer for me.—JOHN TRAPP.

God abhors them worst who adore themselves most.
—WILLIAM SECKER.

---

* Want = lack, be without.

18 AUGUST

COMMENDATION

The praise of them that do well.—1 Pet. 2:14.
Now I praise you, brethren, … but …—1 Cor. 11:2, 3.

TO commend a man with a 'but' is a wound instead of a commendation.—JOHN TRAPP.

To commend that which is good is the ready way to mend the rest.—THOMAS MANTON.

Only a Christian of strong grace can bear the strong wine of commendation without the spiritual intoxication of pride.
—WILLIAM JENKYN.

To be praised of a praiseless person is no praise.—JOHN TRAPP.

The giver of alms may not, but the receiver of them may, blow a trumpet.—THOMAS FULLER.

Christ could discern gold in ore.—RICHARD SIBBES.

Admiration is the overplus* of expectation.—JOHN TRAPP.

---

* Overplus = surplus or excess.

19 August

POVERTY AND GODLINESS

I will also leave in the midst of thee an afflicted and poor people, and they shall trust in the name of the Lord.—Zeph. 3:12.

POOR persons, even under rags, may be very like God.
—JOHN OWEN.

They which are *poor* of *wealth*, may be *rich* in *faith*, and a master's *servant* may be the Lord's *freeman*.

—CHRISTOPHER NESSE.

The poor widow never was better off than when the prophet kept house for her.—WILLIAM GURNALL.

The world's poor are miserable, because dejected in their poverty; the devil's poor cursed, because proud in their poverty; God's poor only blessed, as having nothing yet possessing all things.—JOHN BOYS.

Poverty is a friend to prayer.—GEORGE SWINNOCK.

In that fire in which the chaff is burnt, gold sparkleth.
—THOMAS MANTON.

A poor soul may be a rich Christian.—JOHN TRAPP.

20 August

TRUTH

Say nothing but the truth.—2 Chron. 18:15.
Speak ye every man the truth.—Zech. 8:16.
Truth is fallen in the street.—Isa. 59:14.

TRUTH must be spoken however it be taken.—JOHN TRAPP.

Truth reforms as well as informs.—WILLIAM JENKYN.

Truth is like our first parents, most beautiful when naked.
—JOHN TRAPP.

Truth finds few that love her *gratis*.—WILLIAM GURNALL.

Truth seldom goes without a scratched face.—JOHN TRAPP.

Truth, in what appearance soever, doth never contradict itself.
—STEPHEN CHARNOCK.

Truth is a good mistress; but he that follows her too close at heels, may hap to have his teeth struck out.—JOHN TRAPP.

Truth in the head without holy courage makes a man like the sword fish, he hath a sword in his head but no heart to use it.—WILLIAM GURNALL.

21 August

CONFESSION

He shall confess that he hath sinned.—Lev. 5:5.
I acknowledge my sin unto thee.—Psa. 32:5.
I have sinned.—Exod. 9:27; Num. 22:34; Josh. 7:20;
1 Sam. 15:24; Matt. 27:4.

CONFESSION is verbal humiliation.—RICHARD SIBBES.

Judas confessed himself to a priest, and yet went and hanged himself.—JOHN TRAPP.

Many blush to confess their faults who never blush to commit them.—WILLIAM SECKER.

Confession is, as it were, the vomit of the soul.
—THOMAS MANTON.

Thou hast filled God's bag with thy sins, and hast thou no tears for his bottle?—GEORGE SWINNOCK.

Many decline sin through all the cases, yet they will not acknowledge their sin in any case.—JOHN BOYS.

The way to cover our sin is to uncover it by confession.
—RICHARD SIBBES.

22 August

GRACE AND GIFT

Covet earnestly the best gifts: and yet ...—1 Cor. 12:31.

GIFTS are the gold that beautifies the temple; grace is as the temple that sanctifies the gold.—JOHN FLAVEL.

A drop of grace is worth a sea of gifts.—WILLIAM JENKYN.

Those who want grace and true sanctity may notwithstanding have manners and good civility.—THOMAS FULLER.

One dram of grace is worth more than a world of gifts.
—GEORGE SWINNOCK.

When gifts are in their eminency, sin may be in its prevalency.
—THOMAS ADAMS.

Gifts are but as *dead graces*; but graces are *living gifts*.
—CHRISTOPHER NESSE.

Gifts are (as it were) God's shipping, to convey his treasures of grace upon the shore of his people's souls.
—WILLIAM JENKYN.

23 AUGUST

PRAISE

It is good to sing praises unto our God; for it is pleasant; and praise is comely.—Psa. 147:1.

THERE are some things good but not pleasant, as afflictions; some things are pleasant but not good, as sin; and some things may be both good and pleasant.—NEHEMIAH ROGERS.

The peppercorn of praise is all the rent God looks for.
—JOHN TRAPP.

Praise is a soul in flower.—THOMAS WATSON.

The servants of the Lord are to sing his praises in this life to the world's end; and in the next life, world without end.
—JOHN BOYS.

Praise should conclude that work which prayer began.
—WILLIAM JENKYN.

If the heart be glad the tongue is glib.—JOHN HUME.

Praise is the quit-rent* we pay to God; while God renews our lease, we must renew our rent.—THOMAS WATSON.

---

* Quit-rent = a rent, typically a small one, paid in lieu of services which might otherwise be required.

24 August

THE BREVITY AND BOUNDS OF TIME

The angel ... sware by him that liveth for ever and ever ... that there should be time no longer.—Rev. 10:5, 6.

TIME is fluid, but eternity is stable.—STEPHEN CHARNOCK.

The longest life reached not to a thousand years, and that is not a day unto God.—THOMAS ADAMS.

As time is but a slip of eternity, so it will end in eternity.
—STEPHEN CHARNOCK.

The sand of our life runneth as fast, though the hour-glass be set in the sunshine of prosperity, as in the gloomy shade of affliction.—THOMAS FULLER.

Time cannot be infinite.—STEPHEN CHARNOCK.

The world began with time and time with it.—THOMAS ADAMS.

Of all other possessions, two may be had together; but two moments of time cannot be possessed together.
—JOHN TRAPP.

25 August

KEEPING THE HEART

Keep thy heart above all that thou guardest; for out of it are the issues of life.—Prov. 4:23. (R.V. Margin.)

HEART-WORK is weighty and difficult work; an error there may cost you your souls.—JOHN FLAVEL.

The spring and wheels of the clock must be mended before the hand of the dial will stand right.—STEPHEN CHARNOCK.

A rule of three, (1) our affections, (2) our words, (3) our actions.
—NEHEMIAH ROGERS.

Look we well to our affections, for by these maids Satan still wooeth the mistress.—JOHN TRAPP.

Our hearts are slippery commodities.—THOMAS GOODWIN.

A careless eye is an index to a graceless heart.—WILLIAM SECKER.

26 August

CONSCIENCE

The testimony of our conscience.—2 Cor. 1:12.

CONSCIENCE is God's spy and man's overseer.
—JOHN TRAPP.

Conscience is God's vicar.—RICHARD SIBBES.

It's hard to be in office and not put conscience out of office.
—THOMAS WATSON.

Conscience is a castle that no batteries but what God raiseth against it can shake.—WILLIAM GURNALL.

Conscience is to the soul as the stomach is to the body.
—THOMAS ADAMS.

Conscience, the domestic chaplain.—JOHN TRAPP.

Conscience is the deputy-deity in the little world, man.
—GEORGE SWINNOCK.

No flattery can heal a bad conscience, so no slander can hurt a good one.—THOMAS WATSON.

27 August

THE SINGLENESS OF LOYALTY

No servant can serve two masters.—Luke 16:13.

He commands the heart, that is master of its love.
—WILLIAM GURNALL.

The devil's stamp is none of God's badge.
—STEPHEN CHARNOCK.

One heaven holdeth not Michael and the dragon in peace; nor one house the Ark and Dagon.—JOHN KING.

The body has two eyes, but the soul must have but one.
—WILLIAM SECKER.

God must be served truly, that there be no halting; and totally, that there be no halving.—JOHN TRAPP.

Christ will bear no equal, and Satan no superior, and therefore hold in with both you cannot.—WILLIAM GURNALL.

Diversity of religion is against the essence of God, which is but one.—CHRISTOPHER NESSE.

28 August

OLD AGE AND YOUTH

The hoary head is a crown of glory,
if it be found in the way of righteousness.—Prov. 16:31.
Let no man despise thy youth.—1 Tim. 4:12.

HE that will be old long, must be old while he is young.
—THOMAS ADAMS.

Youth seasoned with the fear of God is not easily despised.
—JOHN TRAPP.

Green wood and old logs meet in one fire.—THOMAS BROOKS.

If youth be sick of the *will-nots*, old age is in danger of dying of the *shall-nots*.—WILLIAM SECKER.

None can be too young to amend, that is old enough to die.
—THOMAS ADAMS.

'Tis a thousand pities, that those who have one foot in the grave would live as if the other were in hell.—JOHN FLAVEL.

The old cannot live long, the young may die very quickly.
—JOHN RAINOLDS.

'Twixt the dotage of old men and the prejudice of young men the Commonwealth faileth.—CHRISTOPHER NESSE.

29 AUGUST

SAINTS

The saints that are in the earth.—Psa. 16:3.
As he is, so are we in this world.—1 John 4:17.

GODLINESS is nothing but God-likeness.
—GEORGE SWINNOCK.

True saints are the world's rarities.—JOHN FLAVEL.

The saints are the walking pictures of God.—THOMAS WATSON.

Liking is founded in *likeness.*

Godliness is the constitution of a real Christian.
—GEORGE SWINNOCK.

Every true Christian is a Theophilus.—JOHN BOYS.

Saints are princes in all lands.—GEORGE SWINNOCK.

Love and likeness to God are inseparable.—JOHN OWEN.

Enoch walked so little like the world, that his stay was little in the world.—JOSEPH CARYL.

30 August

TROUBLE SAFER THAN PROSPERITY

Before I was afflicted I went astray: but now have I kept thy word.—
Psa. 119:67.

JONAH was asleep in the ship, but at prayer in the whale's belly.—THOMAS WATSON.

Better be preserved in brine than rot in honey.—JOHN TRAPP.

Israel was safer in the brick-kilns of Egypt than in the plains of Moab.—WILLIAM JENKYN.

Manasseh's chain was more profitable to him than his crown.
—THOMAS BROOKS.

Thou art beaten that thou mayest be better.—JOHN BUNYAN.

While the wicked are kept in sugar, the godly are often kept in brine.—THOMAS WATSON.

Better be pruned to grow than cut up to burn.—JOHN TRAPP.

31 August

COVETOUSNESS AND ERROR

They ... ran greedily after the error of Balaam for reward.—Jude 11.
Enticing unstedfast souls; having a heart exercised in covetousness.
—2 Pet. 2:14. (R.V.)

THE covetousness of heretics is the companion, fuel, mother, nurse of their heresies.—WILLIAM JENKYN.

If yellow angels make up the match, the evil angels will be at the marriage.—GEORGE SWINNOCK.

To be poor in purse is his fear, to be poor in spirit is none of his desire.—THOMAS ADAMS.

Silver is in the sack's mouth of every popish error. Covetousness swallows down any lie.—WILLIAM JENKYN.

Hugo Cardinalis said the devil had two daughters, Avarice and Luxury: the former whereof he had married to the Jews, the latter to the Gentiles; but now, saith he, the priests have taken away both of them from their right husband, and made use of them for their own.—JOHN TRAPP.

1 September

GUILT AND SHAME

He hath sinned, and is guilty.—Lev. 6:4.
I hid myself.—Gen. 3:10.

GUILT is shy of God's presence.—THOMAS MANTON.

The terrors of God are the effects of guilt.
—STEPHEN CHARNOCK.

The burden of sin is the wrath of God.—EDWARD MARBURY.

Better thy house be haunted with devils than thy soul with guilt.—THOMAS WATSON.

Guilt is to danger what fire is to gunpowder.—JOHN FLAVEL.

Guiltiness is ever clamourous, and the most lewd are the most loud.—JOHN TRAPP.

It is guilt which makes us shy of God.—GEORGE SWINNOCK.

Shame is fear of a just reproof.—THOMAS MANTON.

2 September

HOSPITALITY

Given to hospitality.—Rom. 12:13.
The barbarous people shewed us no little kindness: for they kindled a fire and received us every one.—Acts 28:2.

THOUGH the sun of charity rise at home, yet it should always set abroad.—WILLIAM SECKER.

Hospitality is threefold: for one's family, this of necessity; for strangers, this is courtesy; for the poor, this is charity.
—THOMAS FULLER.

I know no better way to preserve your meal than by parting with your cake.—WILLIAM SECKER.

Lot's guests were his best friends.—THOMAS ADAMS.

Mercy is so good a servant that it will never suffer its master to die a beggar.—WILLIAM SECKER.

Great boast and small roast makes unsavoury mouths.
—HENRY SMITH.

3 September

INFLUENCE, GOOD AND BAD

They shall not dwell in thy land, lest they make thee sin against me.
—Exod. 23:33.

What have I to do any more with idols? I have answered, and will regard him.—Hos. 14:8. (R.V.)

ELISHA could do more with a kiss than his man with a staff.—JOHN TRAPP.

Christians should be like musk among linen.
—THOMAS BROOKS.

Charity, like musk, will discover itself.—GEORGE SWINNOCK.

No wool so coarse but will take some colour.—JOHN TRAPP.

A man that keepeth ill company is like him that walketh in the sun, tanned insensibly.—THOMAS MANTON.

There is little we touch, but we leave the print of our fingers behind.—RICHARD BAXTER.

Opinion sets the price.—JOHN TRAPP.

Man is a creature that is led more by patterns than by precepts.
—GEORGE SWINNOCK.

4 September

ANSWERS TO PRAYER PROMISED

Every one that asketh receiveth; and he that seeketh findeth; and to him that knocketh it shall be opened.—Matt. 7:8.

THE Bible is bespangled with promises made to prayer.
—THOMAS WATSON.

God never denied that soul anything that went as far as heaven to ask it.—JOHN TRAPP.

That soul shall have his will of God, who desires nothing but what God will.—WILLIAM SECKER.

God may deny your wantonness, but not your wants.
—JOHN FLAVEL.

Pure prayers have pure blessings.—THOMAS GOODWIN.

Prayer is a putting the promises into suit.*—JOHN TRAPP.

If you would believe you must crucify the question 'How?'
—MARTIN LUTHER.

---

* Into suit = into petitions to be pleaded before God.

5 September

SELF

In their selfwill.—Gen. 49:6.
Selfwilled.—2 Pet 2:10.

SELF is the most abominable principle that ever was.
—THOMAS GOODWIN.

Self-seeking has been so long pulling the ropes that it has rung the passing-bell* of many nations.—WILLIAM SECKER.

Self is the soul, the spirit of unregeneracy.—THOMAS GOODWIN.

Self is the poise of the unsanctified heart, which biases it and moves it in all its designs and actions.—JOHN FLAVEL.

Sinful self is to be destroyed, and natural self is to be denied.
—WILLIAM SECKER.

Self-love is king in unregenerate hearts.—THOMAS GOODWIN.

Where *self* is the end of our actions, there *Satan* is the rewarder of them.—WILLIAM SECKER.

A self-seeker is a Cato[†] without, but a Nero[‡] within.
—THOMAS BROOKS.

---

* Passing-bell = a bell tolled immediately after a death.

† Cato (the Younger, 95 B.C.–A.D. 46), a Roman politician and statesman who was known for his moral integrity.

‡ Nero (A.D. 37–68) Roman emperor (A.D. 54–68), known for his tyranny and extravagance.

6 September

VAIN THOUGHTS

How long shall thy vain thoughts lodge within thee?—Jer. 4:14.
I hate vain thoughts.—Psa. 119:113.

VAIN thoughts are very sins.—JOHN TRAPP.

Vain thoughts defile the heart as well as *vile* thoughts.
—WILLIAM SECKER.

A disloyal thought is seminal apostasy.—JOHN HOWE.

Ill thoughts are little thieves.—RICHARD SIBBES.

Thoughts are mutineers in the soul, which set open the gates for Satan.—STEPHEN CHARNOCK.

Follow every vain thought with a deep sigh.—JOHN FLAVEL.

It is a sure sign of a base mind, though in high place, to think he can make himself great with anything that is less than himself and win more credit by his garments than his graces.
—JOHN TRAPP.

A vain mind is as bad, and as odious to God, as a vicious life.
—THOMAS MANTON.

7 September

CONSISTENT CONDUCT

And I said, Should such a man as I flee? and who is there, that, being such as I, would go into the temple to save his life? I will not go in.
—Neh. 6:11. (R.V.)

THE consideration of whom I am should teach me what a one I should be.—NEHEMIAH ROGERS.

Let us think ourselves too good for the base service of Satan.
—RICHARD SIBBES.

A good life is a good fence against fear.—EDWARD MARBURY.

Eagles must not stoop to catch flies.—GEORGE SWINNOCK.

It is not safe wading far in a questionable water.
—NEHEMIAH ROGERS.

A good name is a thread tied about the finger, to make us mindful of the errand we came into the world to do for our Master.—WILLIAM JENKYN.

We live not to live; our life is not the end in itself, but the praise of the Giver.—RICHARD SIBBES.

8 September

DRESS

And the Lord God made for Adam and for his wife coats of skins, and clothed them.—Gen. 3:21. (R.V.)

THE worst apparel, saith one, is nature's garment; the best but folly's garnish.—JOHN TRAPP.

Clothes and company do oftentimes tell tales in a mute but significant language.—THOMAS BROOKS.

Every clout will cover our sores, but the finest silk will not cover our sins.—HENRY SMITH.

Pearls grace a garment, but it were a strange garment made of nothing but pearls.—THOMAS ADAMS.

Clothes are the ensigns of our sin, and covers of our shame; to be proud of them is as great folly as for a beggar to be proud of his rags, or a thief of his halter.—JOHN TRAPP.

They that plead Rebekah's ornaments for their garish attire, would be loathe to take her office.—JOHN TRAPP.

9 September

LIVING FAITH

The just shall live by his faith.—Hab. 2:4.

FAITH is the life of our lives, the soul that animates the whole body of obedience.—THOMAS MANTON.

Faith is a quickening grace, the vital artery of the soul.
—THOMAS WATSON.

We live by faith, and faith lives by exercise.—WILLIAM GURNALL.

Wheresoever thou art maimed, let thy faith be sound.
—THOMAS ADAMS.

The soul is the life of the body, faith is the life of the soul, Christ is the life of faith.—JOHN FLAVEL.

Faith is not always alike lively; but, where it is true, it is always living.—THOMAS MANTON.

All the Christian's strength and comfort is fetched without doors, and he hath none to send on his errand but faith.
—WILLIAM GURNALL.

10 September

ILL-NATURE

He is such a son of Belial, that a man cannot speak to him.
—1 Sam. 25:17.

RUDENESS hath no respect either to sex or condition.
—JOHN TRAPP.

Through the whole city, there is no one so near to me, and yet so far from me as a sullen neighbour.—THOMAS ADAMS.

Some men's churlishness entirely swallows up their charitableness.—WILLIAM SECKER.

A desire to disgrace others never sprang from grace.
—GEORGE SWINNOCK.

All the world cannot keep him up that doth not keep down his own spirit.—THOMAS BROOKS.

A drop or two of vinegar will sour a whole glass of wine.
—THOMAS WATSON.

An unbridled tongue is *vehiculum diaboli*, the chariot of the devil.—EDWARD REYNER.

11 September

GOD—HIS EXISTENCE

I am.—Gen. 17:1.
He is.—Heb. 11:6.
Thou art.—Psa. 90:2.

GOD is his own eternity.—STEPHEN CHARNOCK.

God is; if he were not, nothing could be.
—RICHARD SIBBES.

God is always like himself.—JOHN CALVIN.

We better understand what God is *not*, than what he *is*.
—STEPHEN CHARNOCK.

God, and all that he has made, is not more than God without anything that he has made.—WILLIAM SECKER.

His duration is without succession.—GEORGE SWINNOCK.

The existence of God is the foundation of all religion.
—STEPHEN CHARNOCK.

12 September

KNOWLEDGE AND OBEDIENCE

If ye know these things, happy are ye if ye do them.—John 13:17.

KNOWLEDGE is the eye that must direct the foot of obedience.—THOMAS WATSON.

Knowledge is the mother of obedience, and obedience is the nurse of knowledge; the former breeds the latter, and the latter feeds the former.—JEAN DAILLÉ.

There is no fear of knowing too much, but there is much fear of practising too little.—THOMAS BROOKS.

Divine knowledge is not as the light of the moon to sleep by; but as the light of the sun to work by.—WILLIAM SECKER.

Practice is the soul of knowledge.—THOMAS ADAMS.

Where the right is absolute, the obedience must not be conditional.—GEORGE SWINNOCK.

Knowledge is to be the usher of grace, information in the understanding must go before reformation in the will and affections.—THOMAS FULLER.

13 September

MURMURING

Wherefore doth a living man murmur?—Lam. 3:39. (Margin.)

OUR murmuring is the devil's music.—THOMAS WATSON.

Murmuring is a black garment, and it becomes none so ill as saints.—THOMAS BROOKS.

Murmuring is a slippery way to an irrecoverable bottom.
—THOMAS ADAMS.

The murmurer is his own martyr.—GEORGE SWINNOCK.

Better to be mute than to murmur.—THOMAS WATSON.

Complain *to* God you may, but to complain *of* God you must not.—JOHN FLAVEL.

The frog and the murmurer, both of them are bred of the mud.—THOMAS ADAMS.

Complain without cause, and thou shalt have cause to complain.—THOMAS TAYLOR.

Murmuring often ends in cursing.—THOMAS WATSON.

14 September

SOUL-WINNING

He that winneth souls is wise.—Prov. 11:30.
He that is wise winneth souls. Prov. 11:30. (R.V.)

THE service of the soul is the soul of service.
—WILLIAM JENKYN.

Faith is of Rachel's humour; 'Give me children or else I die!'
—THOMAS ADAMS.

The setting of a soul in joint is a point of skill and dexterity. It is not for every horse-leech to meddle with this art.
—WILLIAM JENKYN.

There is no such cruelty to men's souls as clemency to their sins.
—GEORGE SWINNOCK.

It is a holy impudence to be impudent in calling on people to regard their souls. It is a sinful modesty to prefer courtesy herein before Christianity.—WILLIAM JENKYN.

Mediation needs not be where all is friendly.—RICHARD SIBBES.

It is very good manners in Christianity to stay, and to knock again, though we have knocked more than three times at a sinner's conscience.—WILLIAM JENKYN.

15 SEPTEMBER

FRIENDSHIP

A friend loveth at all times.—Prov. 17:17.

FRIENDSHIP is the *marriage of affections*.
—THOMAS WATSON.

Most unkindnesses among friends grow upon mistakes.
—JOHN TRAPP.

It is pure friendship to will and nil the same things.
—GEORGE SWINNOCK.

It is hard to find a good piece of stuff indeed to make a friend of.—THOMAS GOODWIN.

In friendship there is one soul in two bodies.—RICHARD SIBBES.

Friends unjustly gotten are not long comfortably enjoyed.
—THOMAS FULLER.

He loves his friend best who hates his lusts most.
—GEORGE SWINNOCK.

Let us quarrel with our faults not with our friends.
—JOHN TRAPP.

16 September

THE WORK OF THE MINISTRY

Take heed to the ministry which thou hast received in the Lord, that thou fulfil it.—Col. 4:17.

The work of the ministry.—Eph. 4:12.

THE word *work* forbids loitering, and the word *ministry* lording.—JOHN BOYS.

Ministers may discover but cannot recover lost souls.
—JOHN FLAVEL.

Ministers may, like Noah's carpenters, build an ark to save others and be drowned.—GEORGE SWINNOCK.

Ministers are not cooks but physicians, and therefore should not study to delight the palate but to recover the patient; they must not provide sauce but physic.—JEAN DAILLÉ.

God's mercy is eminently discovered in the institution, and Satan's malice in the opposition, of the ministerial office.
—JOHN FLAVEL.

The ministry will not grace the man; the man may disgrace the ministry.—JOSEPH HALL.

17 September

LITTLE FAITH

And he saith unto them, Why are ye fearful, O ye of little faith?
—Matt. 8:26.

A WEAK hand may receive a rich jewel.—RICHARD SIBBES.

A little faith is faith as a spark of fire is fire.
—THOMAS WATSON.

A divine spark may live in a smoke of doubts without a speedy rising into a flame.—STEPHEN CHARNOCK.

Faith at first standeth but on one weak foot.
—GEORGE SWINNOCK.

A weak faith may receive a strong Christ.—THOMAS WATSON.

Thomas had his faith at his fingers' end.—JOHN BOYS.

Faith may lie asleep in the habit, when it doth not walk about in the act.—STEPHEN CHARNOCK.

18 September

AVAILING PRAYER

The supplication of a righteous man availeth much in its working.
—James 5:16. (R.V.)

The energetic fervent prayer of a righteous man availeth much.

TO an effectual prayer there must concur the intention of the mind and the affections of the heart; else it is not praying but parrotting.—JOHN TRAPP.

There must be fired affections before our prayers will go up.
—WILLIAM JENKYN.

Prayer is the gun we shoot with, fervency is the fire that discharges it, and faith is the bullet that pierces the throne of grace.—JOHN TRAPP.

Prayer will make a man cease from sin, or sin will entice a man to cease from prayer.—JOHN BUNYAN.

Those prayers that awaken God must awaken us.
—THOMAS GOODWIN.

Good prayers never come weeping home.—JOSEPH HALL.

As a man cannot preach without external mission, so not pray without internal motion.—WILLIAM JENKYN.

19 September

MISERY AND MERCY

His soul was grieved for the misery of Israel.—Judg. 10:16.
*Thou shalt forget thy misery,
and remember it as waters that pass away.*—Job 11:16.

WHERE misery passes undiscerned, there mercy passes undesired.—WILLIAM SECKER.

The diocese where mercy visits is very large.—THOMAS WATSON.

Without misery, mercy can never set foot in the world.
—STEPHEN CHARNOCK.

Misery should be a lodestone* of mercy, not a footstool for pride to trample on.—RICHARD SIBBES.

It is a far happier thing to be pitied of God than to be envied of men.—SIR RICHARD BAKER.

A merciful man is God's almoner.—WILLIAM JENKYN.

Unmercifulness is twofold; when we neither give nor forgive.
—THOMAS MANTON.

---

* Lodestone = a magnet.

20 September

CHRIST AND THE PROMISES OF GOD

For all the promises in him are yea; wherefore, also, through him let there be Amen, unto the glory of God by us.
—2 Cor. 1:20. (Calvin's translation.)

THE resurrection of Christ is the Amen of all his promises.
—JOHN BOYS.

We cannot close with Christ without a promise; and we must not close with a promise without Christ.
—THOMAS MANTON.

Though providences may seem to cross one another, they shall never cross God's promises.—STEPHEN CHARNOCK.

The Tyrians tied their god Hercules with a golden chain that he should not remove; God hath tied himself fast to us by his promises.—THOMAS WATSON.

The promise is the marriage-ring on the hand of faith; now we are not married to the ring, but with it to Christ.
—WILLIAM GURNALL.

The promise chains mercies together.—THOMAS BOSTON.

21 September

MODESTY AND UNCLEANNESS

That women adorn themselves in decent apparel, with modesty.
—1 Tim. 2:9. (Calvin's translation.)

MODESTY is the life-guard of chastity.—THOMAS FULLER.

Modesty is the only visible virtue, the chastity of the looks.—THOMAS ADAMS.

Blushing is the colour of virtue displayed by nature in the countenance.—WILLIAM JENKYN.

Innocence hath so clear a complexion that she needs no painting.—THOMAS FULLER.

Lust is a sin of two; if but one party be wise, both escape.
—THOMAS ADAMS.

Let painted faces look in Jezebel's glass, and see how they like themselves.—MATTHEW HENRY.

Uncleanness loves a dark mind, as well as a dark house.
—THOMAS ADAMS.

22 September

DESPAIR AND PRESUMPTION

The speeches of one that is desperate.—Job 6:26.
Ye ... were presumptuous.—Deut. 1:43. (R.V.)

WITHOUT joy we shall despair; without fear presume.
—JOHN BOYS.

The despairing soul deals little better with the promise than the presumptuous sinner with the threatening.
—WILLIAM GURNALL.

Despair is the period of presumption.—WILLIAM JENKYN.

God does not always frown, lest we should be cast into despair. God does not always smile, lest we should be careless and presume.—JOHN OWEN.

Despair is hope stark dead, presumption is hope stark mad.
—THOMAS ADAMS.

To look upon a promise without a precept is the high road to *presumption*; to look upon a precept without a promise is the high road to *desperation*.—WILLIAM SECKER.

23 September

LOVE

*Let us not love in word, neither in tongue;
but in deed and in truth.*—1 John 3:18.

He loves but little who tells how much he loves.
—JOHN BOYS.

Our love, if sound, will be discerned by our fear.
—NEHEMIAH ROGERS.

A verbal kindness costs little and helps little.—JAMES JANEWAY.

No such picklock to open the heart as love.
—WILLIAM GURNALL.

Affection without action is like Rachel, beautiful but barren.
—JOHN TRAPP.

The best wedge to drive out an old love is to take in a new.
—THOMAS FULLER.

Of love there be two principal offices: one to give, another to forgive.—JOHN BOYS.

24 September

MELANCHOLY

Few and evil have the days of the years of my life been.—Gen. 47:9.

MELANCHOLY clothes the mind in sable.
—THOMAS WATSON.

He that looks through a green glass sees no other colour.
—THOMAS ADAMS.

One calls melancholy *balneum diaboli*, the devil's bath; he bathes himself with delight in such a person.
—THOMAS WATSON.

Drooping spirits may be believers.—STEPHEN CHARNOCK.

A melancholy person tempts the devil to tempt him.
—THOMAS WATSON.

A repining submission is a partial opposition to the will of God.
—STEPHEN CHARNOCK.

Melancholy gives the devil great advantages; it pulls off the chariot wheels.—THOMAS WATSON.

25 September

HERESY

False teachers ... who privily shall bring in damnable heresies.
—2 Pet. 2:1.

HERESY is the leprosy in the head.—JOHN TRAPP.

A man may go to hell as well for heresy as adultery.
—THOMAS WATSON.

No heresy so foul but in show produceth some scripture for itself.—THOMAS GOODWIN.

Tertullian, speaking of some heretics' manner of preaching, saith, they teach by persuading, and not persuade by teaching.—WILLIAM GURNALL.

Error damns as well as vice; the one pistols, the other poisons.
—THOMAS WATSON.

A humble man will never be a heretic.—JOHN TRAPP.

An evil ear maketh an heretic.—HENRY SMITH.

26 September

JUDGING OTHERS

As the Lord liveth, the man that hath done this thing shall surely die.
—2 Sam. 12:5.

How severe justicers we can be to our own crimes in others' persons!—NEHEMIAH ROGERS.

If thou must needs be a judge, then pray sit upon your own bench.—WILLIAM SECKER.

If God should have no more mercy on us than we have charity one to another, what would become of us?
—THOMAS FULLER.

We must take heed we neither make censure's whip nor charity's cloak too long.—JOHN TRAPP.

The judgment hath best view of things when they are carried in a third person, and is not so blinded and perverted as in our own case.—THOMAS MANTON.

They are fittest to find fault, in whom there is no fault to be found.—WILLIAM SECKER.

We must not prove the faith from the persons, but the persons from the faith.—RICHARD STOCK.

27 September

FAITH AND WORKS IN JUSTIFICATION

We reckon therefore that a man is justified by faith apart from the works of the law.—Rom. 3:28. (R.V.)

IF good works offer to crowd into our justification, let us be so bold as to shut the door against them.—THOMAS FULLER.

Abraham was justified by works before men; but, before God, it was the righteousness of Christ, wherein, by faith, he shrouded himself.—ELISHA COLES.

We are not justified by doing good works, but being justified we then do good.—WILLIAM JENKYN.

Out of the point of justification works cannot be sufficiently commended; into the cause of justification they must not be admitted.—THOMAS ADAMS.

There is a double degree of justification: one in our conscience now, another at the day of judgment.—RICHARD SIBBES.

Faith justifies the person, and works justify his faith.
—ELISHA COLES.

28 September

SINCERITY

Be sincere and without offence.—Phil. 1:10.
Not as the many ... but as of sincerity.—2 Cor. 2:17. (R.V.)

SINCERITY is the salt which seasons every sacrifice.
—STEPHEN CHARNOCK.

To be true to convictions is the life of sincerity.—JOHN OWEN.

Sincerity is the truth of all grace.—WILLIAM SECKER.

Sincerity shields from hell but not from slander.
—THOMAS WATSON.

He that is sincere, is sincere in all places, and at all times.
—RICHARD SIBBES.

The greatest flourishes and appearances of hypocrisy cannot reach the excellency of the least dram of sincerity.
—WILLIAM JENKYN.

He grieves truly that weeps without a witness.
—GEORGE SWINNOCK.

The gloss of profession without sincerity will off in a storm.
—THOMAS ADAMS.

29 September

HOLY JOY

Let us rejoice in hope of the glory of God. And not only so, but let us also rejoice in our tribulations ... and not only so, but we also rejoice in God.—Rom. 5:2, 3, 11. (R.V.)

JOY cannot be suppressed in the heart, but it must be expressed with the tongue.—JOHN HUME.

In our sufferings for Christ there is joy; not so when we suffer for our sins.—JOHN TRAPP.

Here joy begins to enter into us, *there* we enter into joy.
—THOMAS WATSON.

Holy joy is the oil to the wheels of our obedience.
—MATTHEW HENRY.

The godly make it Hilary Term* all the year.—JOHN BOYS.

Salvation is a happy security and a secure happiness.
—WILLIAM JENKYN.

Happiness is nothing but the Sabbath of our thoughts.
—GEORGE SWINNOCK.

Those that look to be happy must first look to be holy.
—RICHARD SIBBES.

---

* Hilary Term = Spring term at Oxford University (after Hilary of Poitiers (d. c. A.D. 367; festival 13 January). A playful pun on 'Hilary' (i.e. hilarious = cheerful)

30 September

PROMISES AND PRAYER

Thou art God, ... and thou hast promised this good thing unto thy servant.—2 Samuel 7:28. (R.V.)

OUR Saviour joins the promise and the petition together; the promise to encourage the petition, and the petition to enjoy the promise.—STEPHEN CHARNOCK.

The promises are the cork to keep faith from sinking in prayer.
—THOMAS WATSON.

Faith melts promises into arguments, as the soldier doth lead into bullets.—WILLIAM GURNALL.

The being of God may as well fail as the promise of God.
—TIMOTHY CRUSO.

Promises are not damps, but incentive and guides to prayer; they are to inflame us, not to cool us.

—STEPHEN CHARNOCK.

The promises are not made to strong faith but to true.
—THOMAS WATSON.

There is no way how God can be conceived to contract a debt to his creature, but by promise.—WILLIAM GURNALL.

1 October

THE NATURAL MAN

The natural man.—1 Cor. 2:14.
The old man.—Eph. 4:22.

THE natural man, like Zacchaeus, is too low of stature to see Jesus.—GEORGE SWINNOCK.

Any natural man, he is iron to God and wax to the devil.
—RICHARD SIBBES.

Nature never sets up a light to discover its own deformities.
—WILLIAM JENKYN.

Self is the chief end of every natural man.
—STEPHEN CHARNOCK.

The natural man turns from one custom and posture to another, but never turns off.—ROBERT LEIGHTON.

Embellished nature is nature still.—JOHN FLAVEL.

The principle of a natural man in his religious actions is artificial.
—STEPHEN CHARNOCK.

He who is and continues no more than a man, had better never have been so much as a man.—WILLIAM JENKYN.

2 October

RESULTS OF CONVERSION

*Instead of the thorn shall come up the fir tree,
and instead of the brier shall come up the myrtle tree.*—Isa. 55:13.

IF a man be hot and earnest in his temper, grace takes not away his heart, but turns it into zeal.—STEPHEN CHARNOCK.

It is a rare piece of Christian wisdom to turn those passions of the soul which most predominate into spiritual channels, to turn natural anger into spiritual zeal, natural mirth into holy cheerfulness, and natural fear into a holy dread and awe of God.—JOHN FLAVEL.

Conversion, like the shipman's fatal star, is never seen but before the wreck and death of sin.—GEORGE SWINNOCK.

God can change a filthy sinner into a washen saint.
—DAVID DICKSON.

The prodigal by his change of mind had a chance of refreshment; robes for rags, and a fatted calf for husks.
—STEPHEN CHARNOCK.

3 OCTOBER

DUTY

The duty of every day.—Ezra 3:4.

DUTY fits the heart for duty.—GEORGE SWINNOCK.

Duties can never have too much of our diligence, or too little of our confidence.—WILLIAM SECKER.

No duty can be spiritual that hath a carnal aim.
—STEPHEN CHARNOCK.

Duties are used by many as a sleepy sop to allay the rage of conscience.—THOMAS MANTON.

Look upon duties as the gallery of communion in which you walk with God.—JOHN FLAVEL.

Eternity cannot free us from duty.—STEPHEN CHARNOCK.

Never did the holy God give a privilege where he did not expect a duty.—JOSEPH HALL.

Stated time is a hedge to duty, and defends it against many temptations to omission.—RICHARD BAXTER.

4 October

THE VALUE OF FAITH

Precious faith.—2 Pet. 1:1.

RECKON one grain of grace more worth than all the gold of Ophir, one remnant of faith beyond all the gorgeous and gay attire of the world.—JOHN TRAPP.

Faith gives a propriety in any attribute it looks upon, and draws on the virtues thereof for itself.—ELISHA COLES.

Lose not thy faith, and thou shalt never lose Christ.
—THOMAS ADAMS.

Faith is a sworn officer to the great King, and has a key for every lock that is fit to be opened; it forces nothing, but where it cannot enter, it stays without and waits a better season.
—ELISHA COLES.

Faith doth more in religion than the mouth.—HENRY SMITH.

One grain of faith is more precious than a pound of knowledge.
—JOSEPH HALL.

As faith is the choicest grace, so that which is opposite to it must be the greatest sin.—STEPHEN CHARNOCK.

5 OCTOBER

GRACE AND GLORY

The Lord will give grace and glory.—Psa. 84:11.

GRACE is young glory.—ALEXANDER PEDEN.

Grace is the earnest-penny* of glory.—RICHARD SIBBES.

Never stop nor stay in grace till thou comest to glory.
—THOMAS FULLER.

Grace is glory inchoate,† glory is grace consummate.
—GEORGE SWINNOCK.

Grace is gold in the leaf, and glory is gold in plates.
—JOHN BUNYAN.

Grace and glory differ very little; the one is the seed, the other is the flower; grace is glory militant, glory is grace triumphant.
—THOMAS BROOKS.

The growth of grace is glory.—RICHARD SIBBES.

---

* Earnest-penny = a penny given in token of a bargain made; a pledge.
† Inchoate = just begun, not fully formed or developed; unfinished.

6 October

LIBERALITY TO THE POOR

He that giveth unto the poor shall not lack: but he that hideth his eyes shall have many a curse.—Prov. 28:27.

IF there be in your bags but one shilling that should have been the poor's, that shilling shall be the consumption of all its fellows.—THOMAS ADAMS.

The minister's chest is the poor man's box.—JOHN TRAPP.

It is an easy matter to be liberal on other men's purses.
—THOMAS GRANGER.

Power to help, without will to assist, is a dry chip.
—STEPHEN CHARNOCK.

The poor man's hand is Christ's bank.—JOHN TRAPP.

Let thy fast be the poor's feast.—THOMAS ADAMS.

7 October

FORGIVENESS

Forgive, if ye have ought against any.—Mark 11:25.
Dearly beloved, avenge not yourselves.—Rom. 12:19.

WHILST wrongs are remembered they are not remitted. He forgives not that forgets not.—JOHN TRAPP.

Jacob makes his prayers to a heavenly Father, and yet presents his gifts to an angry brother.—WILLIAM SECKER.

By revenge thou canst but satisfy a lust, but by forgiveness thou shalt conquer a lust.—JOHN FLAVEL.

He that demands mercy, and shows none, ruins the bridge over which he himself is to pass.—THOMAS ADAMS.

They that believe that they have a God to right them will not so much wrong themselves as to avenge their own wrongs.
—JOHN FLAVEL.

If the offender say, I repent, the offended may say, I remit.
—GEORGE SWINNOCK.

The best remedy against injuries is forgetfulness.—JOHN KING.

8 October

PARENTS AND CHILDREN

I know him, that he will command his children.—Gen. 18:19.
Children, obey your parents in the Lord.—Eph. 6:1.

SO must the son please him that begot him, that he displease not him that created him.—THOMAS FULLER.

Children, like the conclusion of a syllogism, follow the worst part.—CHRISTOPHER NESSE.

Some parents, like Eli, bring up their children to bring down their house.—GEORGE SWINNOCK.

Absalom signifies his father's peace; but he that was so called proved his father's trouble.—THOMAS ADAMS.

Our children are the Danes* that drive us out of the country.
—JOHN TRAPP.

As for those parents who will not use the rod upon their children, I pray God he useth not their children as a rod for them.—THOMAS FULLER.

---

* Danes = Vikings.

9 October

NEMESIS

As I have done, so God hath requited me.—Judg. 1:7.
The wicked is snared in the work of his own hands.—Psa. 9:16.

NADAB offers strange fire, and suffers strange.
—THOMAS ADAMS.

In the same field where Absalom raised battle against his father, stood the oak that was his gibbet.—WILLIAM COWPER.

Haman feasted with the king one day, and made a feast for the crows the next.—THOMAS BROOKS.

Jerusalem will prove a burdensome stone to all that trouble themselves with it.—ELISHA COLES.

The Lord hath determined that who opposeth *his friends* must be deceived and plagued by *their friends*.—JOHN RAINOLDS.

That which a man spits against heaven, shall fall back on his own face.—THOMAS ADAMS.

That tribe perished first, that lost the tabernacle first.
—CHRISTOPHER NESSE.

Tyrants seldom go to their graves in peace.—THOMAS HALL.

10 October

RICHES AND SALVATION

The breadth of the gate was three cubits on this side, and three cubits on that side.—Ezek. 40:48.

Strait is the gate.—Matt. 7:14.

How hardly shall they that have riches enter into the kingdom of God!—Mark 10:23.

SIX cubits!* What is sixteen cubits to him who would enter in here with all the world on his back.—JOHN BUNYAN.

Some mariners, out of love to their lading, have lost their lives.
—GEORGE SWINNOCK.

The two poles shall sooner meet than the love of God and the love of money.—JOHN TRAPP.

It's better being rich in grace than rich in purse.
—JAMES JANEWAY.

Where there is no want, there is usually much wantonness.
—JOHN FLAVEL.

A rich man is a rare dish at heaven's table.
—GEORGE SWINNOCK.

Religion brought forth wealth, and the daughter devoured the mother.—JOHN TRAPP.

* A cubit = a measurement of 18 inches, or 44 centimetres.

11 October

FOLLY AND SIN OF SLANDER

He that uttereth a slander, is a fool.—Prov. 10:18.
The end of his talk is mischievous madness.—Eccles. 10:13.
Thou shalt not raise [margin, *receive*] *a false report.*—Exod. 23:1.

AN evil speaker is his own scourge.—WILLIAM JENKYN.

He that shoots at the clothes cannot say he meant no ill to the man.—THOMAS ADAMS.

The tale-bearer hath the devil in his tongue; the receiver in his ear.—JOHN BOYS.

Of whom thou canst say no good, say nothing. Of those of whom thou canst say some good, say no bad.
—THOMAS FULLER.

Tale bearer – seldom such a pedlar opens his pack of wares, but some or other will buy.—WILLIAM JENKYN.

The thief doth send one only to the devil, the adulterer two; but the slanderer hurteth three; himself, the party to whom, and the party of whom he telleth his tale.—JOHN BOYS.

12 October

CHRIST AND THE SOUL

For I have espoused you to one husband, that I may present you as a chaste virgin to Christ.—2 Cor. 11:2.

TRUE love to Christ is conjugal.—WILLIAM GURNALL.

Christ married our nature that we might be married to him by his Spirit.—RICHARD SIBBES.

In marriage *error personae** makes a nullity.
—NEHEMIAH ROGERS.

Consent makes the match.—THOMAS GOODWIN.

He that takes possession *of* us on earth, takes possession *for* us in heaven.—WILLIAM SECKER.

Ministers are Christ's paranymphs.†—NEHEMIAH ROGERS.

He hath got but a little of Christ, that fears to get too much.
—THOMAS TAYLOR.

---

* *Error personae* = a mistake respecting the identity of a person.
† A friend going with a bridegroom to fetch home the bride; also used of the bridesmaid conducting the bride to the bridegroom

13 October

STRIFE

The beginning of strife is as when one letteth out water: therefore leave off contention, before there be quarrelling.—Prov. 17:14. (R.V.)

CONTENTION is sooner stirred than stinted.
—JOHN TRAPP.

Dissolution is the daughter of dissension.—THOMAS BROOKS.

Seedsmen sow not in a storm.—JOHN TRAPP.

It is not controversy we have to dread so much as the spirit of controversy.—RICHARD TREFFRY, JR.

The devil loves to fish in troubled waters.—JOHN TRAPP.

Satan lives like a salamander, in fires of contention.
—JOHN FLAVEL.

Divisions are Satan's powder plot to blow up religion.
—THOMAS WATSON.

The second blow makes the fray.—JOHN TRAPP.

14 October

USE OF CHRISTIAN LIBERTY

Use not liberty for an occasion to the flesh.—Gal. 5:13.
Not using your liberty for a cloke of maliciousness.—1 Pet. 2:16.

GOSPEL liberty is a liberty from sin, not to sin.
—THOMAS HALL.

A Christian hath not liberty to riot in his opinion.
—RICHARD SIBBES.

The note that comes too near in the margin, will skip into the text at the next impression.—THOMAS ADAMS.

To argue from mercy to sin is the devil's logic.—JAMES JANEWAY.

That must needs break which is stretched further than God intended it.—THOMAS FULLER.

He that will do all he may, will quickly do what he may not.
—GEORGE SWINNOCK.

How many on account of free tongues have chained feet.
—THOMAS ADAMS.

15 October

GOOD CONSCIENCE

A good conscience and … faith unfeigned.—1 Tim. 1:5.

FAITH and a good conscience are hope's two wings.
—WILLIAM GURNALL.

Cleanse your conscience, and your faith will be out of danger.
—WILLIAM JENKYN.

A good conscience is a Christian's fort-royal.
—THOMAS WATSON.

A good conscience is the inseparable attendant of faith.
—JOHN CALVIN.

A quiet conscience never produced an unquiet conversation.
—JOHN FLAVEL.

If faith be the jewel, a good conscience is the cabinet in which it is kept.—WILLIAM GURNALL.

Bee-masters tell us that those are the best hives that make the most noise. Sure it is that that is the best conscience that suffers not a man to sleep in sin.—JOHN TRAPP.

16 October

HEART AND LIFE

As he thinketh in his heart, so is he.—Prov. 23:7.
A sound heart is the life of the flesh.—Prov. 14:30.

AS the image on the seal is stamped upon the wax, so the thoughts of the heart are printed upon the actions.
—STEPHEN CHARNOCK.

What impress is left upon the wax must needs be in the seal much more.—THOMAS GOODWIN.

Life atheism is but the daughter of heart atheism.
—JEAN DAILLÉ.

The heart of man is his worst part before it is regenerate, and the best afterwards.—JOHN FLAVEL.

There is a concert of all the members when the heart is in tune.—HENRY SMITH.

Man's practices are the best indexes of their principles.
—STEPHEN CHARNOCK.

The body may be a recluse and the heart a wanderer.
—THOMAS ADAMS.

17 October

INCONSISTENCY

Thou that preachest a man should not steal, dost thou steal?
—Rom. 2:21.

IT is foolish to pray against sin and then sin against prayer.
—JOHN TRAPP.

Eyes that may be floodgates to pour out tears, should not be casements* to let in lusts.—WILLIAM SECKER.

What! at peace with the Father and at war with his children? It cannot be!—JOHN FLAVEL.

Worldliness and Christianity are two such ends as never meet.
—NEHEMIAH ROGERS.

A finite duration is inconsistent with infinite perfection.
—STEPHEN CHARNOCK.

God likes not fair words that come out of a foul mouth.
—CHRISTOPHER NESSE.

No Christian but condemns this vice (covetousness), and yet this vice shall condemn many Christians.—THOMAS ADAMS.

---

* Casements = windows.

18 October

THE MEANS OF GRACE

The assembling of ourselves together.—Heb. 10:25.

MEANS must be neither trusted nor neglected.
—JOHN TRAPP.

Many live all their days under the means of grace that never get one dram of grace in the use of the means.
—GEORGE SWINNOCK.

They that stay in the means are like a foolish workman that contenteth himself with the having of tools.
—THOMAS MANTON.

Promises do not exclude, but imply the use of means.
—JOHN FLAVEL.

Neither be idle in the means, nor make an idol of the means.
—WILLIAM SECKER.

It is no matter what the pipe is, whether gold or lead, so the water be the water of life.—STEPHEN CHARNOCK.

Religion is careful; but a foolish scrupulosity and servile awe argue bondage.—THOMAS MANTON.

19 October

PROSPERITY AND ADVERSITY

*In the day of prosperity be joyful,
but in the day of adversity consider.*—Eccles. 7:14.

THEY buckle in adversity that bore their heads high in prosperity.—JOHN TRAPP.

Comforts are not found in adversity that were not sought for in prosperity.—RICHARD SIBBES.

When Joseph was governor of Egypt, it is said that he knew his brethren, but his brethren knew not him; but nowadays it happeneth clean contrary.—THOMAS FULLER.

Pride is a salamander that can live in the fire of suffering.
—WILLIAM GURNALL.

No man must look so high that he overlook his brother.
—THOMAS ADAMS.

It is hard to keep a low spirit with a high lot.
—THOMAS BOSTON.

To see a man humble under prosperity, is one of the greatest rarities in the world.—JOHN FLAVEL.

20 October

RELIGION

Pure religion and undefiled before God and the Father is this, To visit the fatherless and widows in their affliction, and to keep himself unspotted from the world.—James 1:27.

THE life of religion is in the Life.—JOHN OWEN.

The object matter of all religion is reduced to *credenda* and *agenda*.*—THOMAS GOODWIN.

Philosophy seeks after truth; divinity only finds it; religion improves it.—JOHN TRAPP.

We know no more of religion than we love; and we love no more than we do.—RICHARD SIBBES.

Religion is as requisite as reason to complete a man.
—STEPHEN CHARNOCK.

Show your piety by your pity.—THOMAS WATSON.

A poor servant may credit religion as well as a rich master.
—GEORGE SWINNOCK.

There may be many carcasses and forms of religion, but there is but one life.—CHRISTOPHER NESSE.

---

* *Credenda* = things to be believed; *agenda* = things to be done.

21 October

WILLING SERVICE

Whatsoever ye do, work heartily, as unto the Lord.—Col. 3:23. (R.V.)
Not ... as it were of necessity, but willingly.—Philem. 14.

WILLINGNESS is the oil to the wheel.—WILLIAM JENKYN.

God loves adverbs better than nouns; not praying only but praying well; not doing good but doing it well.
—THOMAS BROOKS.

A deed done is a deed not done, where the manner of the doing confutes and confounds the matter of the deed.
—JOHN FLAVEL.

Kind masters may well expect cheerful servants.
—WILLIAM GURNALL.

In sailing, the hand must be to the stern and the eye to the star.
—RICHARD SIBBES.

Consent as much as may be is no more than should be.
—WILLIAM JENKYN.

The success and sweetness of duty are as dear to a Christian as his two eyes; and both of them must necessarily be lost, if the heart is lost in duty.—JOHN FLAVEL.

22 October

SHEEP AND SWINE

The sow that was washed [is turned] to her wallowing in the mire.
—2 Pet. 2:22.

All we like sheep have gone astray.—Isa. 53:6.

A SWINE that wanders can make better shift to get home to the trough than a sheep can to the fold.—JOHN TRAPP.

A sheep may fall into a ditch, but it is the swine that wallows in it.—WILLIAM GURNALL.

Swine love the mire, therefore the devil loves swine.
—THOMAS ADAMS.

Swine will be cleanly in a fair meadow.—GEORGE SWINNOCK.

A sheep may often slip into a slough, as well as a swine.
—THOMAS BROOKS.

Swine think that sheep have no pasture, because they feed not upon draff as they do.—CHRISTOPHER NESSE.

Swill is good enough for swine.—THOMAS TAYLOR.

A sheep feels the bite of a dog, as well as a swine, though she make no such noise.—JOHN TRAPP.

23 October

THE WILES OF THE DEVIL

The wiles of the devil.—Eph. 6:11.
Satan fashioneth himself into an angel of light.—2 Cor. 11:14. (R.V.)
The liar.—1 John 2:22. (R.V.)

THE devil is a great student in divinity.—WILLIAM GURNALL.

Satan is God's ape.—STEPHEN CHARNOCK.

The devil cannot speak truth, but to gain credit for some lie at the end of it.—WILLIAM GURNALL.

The devil does not care how many sermon pills you take, so long as they do not work upon your conscience.
—THOMAS WATSON.

It is an old policy the devil hath, to jostle out a greater good by a less.—NEHEMIAH ROGERS.

A wicked cause needs a smooth orator, bad ware a pleasing chapman.*—WILLIAM GURNALL.

If men's trades can be called crafts, the devil's trade may be called craft.—HENRY SMITH.

The devil would fain compound with us when he cannot conquer us.—JOHN TRAPP.

* Chapman = pedlar, salesman.

24 October

FRIENDS IN EVIL

The same day Pilate and Herod were made friends together.
—Luke 23:12.

BRIERS and thorns twine more together than good plants.
—THOMAS ADAMS.

The peace of some is rather founded in wrath to the saints, than love among themselves.—WILLIAM GURNALL.

Herod neither loved the Jews, nor the Jews Herod, yet both agree to vex the church.—JOHN BOYS.

The amity of the world is enmity against God.
—GEORGE SWINNOCK.

Better a holy discord than a profane concord.
—THOMAS ADAMS.

Simeon and Levi never did worse than when they agreed best.
—JOHN OWEN.

There is more alliance than affiance in the world.
—THOMAS BROOKS.

25 October

HYPOCRITES

The congregation of hypocrites.—Job 15:34
O ye hypocrites.—Matt. 16:3.

THE hypocrite is like Hosea's dough-baked cake, only hot on the visible side.—THOMAS ADAMS.

A hypocrite, like a bankrupt, the less substance he hath, the more show he maketh.—GEORGE SWINNOCK.

Hypocrites resemble looking-glasses, which present the faces not in them.—WILLIAM SECKER.

Like Eli's sons, they are in white linen, but have scarlet sins.
—THOMAS MANTON.

The hypocrite has much angel without, more devil within. He fries in words, freezes in works; speaks by ells,[*] doth good by inches.—THOMAS ADAMS.

A painted harlot is less dangerous than a painted hypocrite.
—WILLIAM SECKER.

The hypocrite can put on faith's mantle, as the devil did Samuel's.
—THOMAS WATSON.

---

[*] Ells, ell = a cloth measure equal to $1\frac{1}{4}$ yards.

26 October

COVETOUSNESS

Take heed, and beware of covetousness.—Luke 12:15.
Let your turn of mind be free from the love of money.
—Heb. 13:5. (r.v. Margin.)

THOSE that count all good fish that come to net, will in the end catch the devil and all.—JOHN TRAPP.

The prophet and Naaman are parted; only Gehazi could not so take his leave; his heart was nailed up in one of Naaman's portmanteaux* and he must after to fetch it.

—THOMAS ADAMS.

All covet all loss. Earth chokes fire.—JOHN TRAPP.

Covetousness, that dropsy thirst after gold and silver, which is never satisfied.—THOMAS TAYLOR.

Covetousness is a dry drunkenness.—JOHN TRAPP.

He is not a covetous man who lays up something providentially; but he is a covetous man who gives out nothing willingly.

—WILLIAM SECKER.

---

* A portmanteau is a large travelling-bag for carrying clothes.

27 October

TIME

Redeeming the time.—Eph. 5:16.

TIME, the mother of truth.—JOHN TRAPP.

Much time hath much duty.—RICHARD BAXTER.

Time consumeth all things.—THOMAS GRANGER.

What is past cannot be recalled; what is future cannot be insured.
—STEPHEN CHARNOCK.

If we lose our time to repent, we shall repent for ever that we once lost our time.—THOMAS ADAMS.

They that have lost time need to have redeemed time.
—MATTHEW HENRY.

God is choice in keeping the keys of time at his own girdle.
—MATTHEW POOLE.

28 October
FAITH PROVED BY WORKS

I will shew thee my faith by my works.—James 2:18.

JUDGE of the health of thy faith by the pulse of charity.
—THOMAS WATSON.

Faith in the promises works obedience to the precepts.
—GEORGE SWINNOCK.

Good deeds are such things, that no man is saved *for* them, nor *without* them.—THOMAS ADAMS.

The saints of God are sealed inwardly with faith, but outwardly with good works.—JOHN BOYS.

We must come to good works by faith, and not to faith by good works.—WILLIAM GURNALL.

Faith is a queen; let repentance be her usher to go before her, and good works the court that follow her.
—THOMAS ADAMS.

The flesh of a man's body, though it receives its heat from the vitals within, yet helps to preserve the very life of those vitals.—WILLIAM GURNALL.

29 October

THE SINNER'S VERDICT ON HIS LIFE

I have played the fool.—1 Sam. 26:21.

SATAN can never undo a man without himself; but a man may easily undo himself without Satan.
—THOMAS BROOKS.

The whole life of man, until he is converted to Christ, is a ruinous labyrinth of wanderings.—JOHN CALVIN.

No felicity can proceed out of vanity.—THOMAS GRANGER.

A sinner though he be truly a friend to none, yet never is he so great a foe to any as to himself.—WILLIAM JENKYN.

Lot seeks himself, and loses himself and his goods.
—THOMAS BROOKS.

Sinners may see nothing but wealth in the commission, but they shall see nothing but woe in the conclusion of sin.
—WILLIAM JENKYN.

He that will not at hand buy good counsel cheap, shall at the second-hand buy repentance over dear.—THOMAS BROOKS.

30 October

EQUALITY BEFORE GOD

God is no respecter of persons: but in every nation he that feareth him ... is accepted with him.—Acts 10:34, 35.

GOD bringeth all home by weeping-cross.
—GEORGE SWINNOCK.

It is not the dignity of the person that gives efficacy unto faith, but it is faith that makes the person accepted.—JOHN OWEN.

It was the sight of *Naaman's shoe* which made *Elisha* so high in the instep.—THOMAS FULLER.

The earth is the womb whereof all are formed, and the breasts whereof all are fed.—THOMAS GOODWIN.

Where God becomes a donor, man becomes a debtor.
—WILLIAM SECKER.

None are so high as to be above God's precepts; none are so low as to be below his providence.—GEORGE SWINNOCK.

The richest man had as poor a beginning as the meanest; as the poorest will have as rich an end as the wealthiest.
—WILLIAM SECKER.

31 October

SOLITUDE

Hang up the hanging at the court gate.—Exod. 40:8.
Enter into thine inner chamber, and ... shut thy door.
—Matt. 6:6. (R.V.)

SOLITUDE is a release to the soul that was imprisoned in company.—GEORGE SWINNOCK.

See to the *Cinque Ports*[*] if you would keep out the enemy. Shut up the five windows, if you would have the house, the heart, full of light.—JOHN TRAPP.

A man in solitariness may be secure, because he seeth no visible enemies, but he is not therefore safe.—GEORGE SWINNOCK.

Distraction in religion is the destruction of religion.
—THOMAS ADAMS.

Soliloquies are the best disputes.—GEORGE SWINNOCK.

Secret meals are those that make the soul fat.—JOHN TRAPP.

Shut the window that the house may be light.—JOHN FLAVEL.

Believers find rich mines of silver and gold in solitary places.
—GEORGE SWINNOCK.

---

[*] The Confederation of Cinque Ports is a historic series of five coastal towns in Kent and Sussex in south-east England (Hastings, New Romney, Hythe, Dover, Sandwich), originally formed for military and trade purposes.

1 November

THE FALL

By one man sin entered into the world, and death by sin.
—Rom. 5:12.
Cursed is the ground for thy sake.—Gen. 3:17.

ADAM'S fall was the devil's masterpiece.—ELISHA COLES.

The very office of the ministry is an argument of the fall.
—JOHN FLAVEL.

Not only the worst of my sins, but the best of my duties speak me a child of Adam.—WILLIAM BEVERIDGE.

Let us not busy our brains so much to know how original sin came into us, as labour with our heart to know how it should be got out of us.—THOMAS FULLER.

Not a faculty can boast itself like the Pharisee, and say I was not like this or that publican; the waves of sin had gone over the heads of every one of them.—ELISHA COLES.

Man lost not his faculties, but the rectitude of them.
—THOMAS GOODWIN.

The whole world died by a wound in the eye.
—WILLIAM SECKER.

2 November

LIGHT AND DARKNESS

Light excelleth darkness.—Eccles. 2:13.

GOD enlargeth the day to his friends, the night to his enemies.—THOMAS ADAMS.

Sin gets up when the sun goes down.—WILLIAM SECKER.

The night is always the best for the enemy, but the worst for Mansoul.—JOHN BUNYAN.

God provides not only light *in* heaven, but light *to* heaven.
—WILLIAM JENKYN.

A man may follow the light within him to the chambers of utter darkness.—GEORGE SWINNOCK.

The devil would soon put out our candles, if Christ did not carry them in his lantern.—WILLIAM SECKER.

He that is in darkness, discerneth not colours, no more doth the fool things that differ.—THOMAS GRANGER.

The new creation, as well as the old, begins with a *fiat lux.*[*]
—STEPHEN CHARNOCK.

---

[*] 'Let there be light.'

3 November

CHARACTER OF TRUE PRAISE

Sing ye praises with understanding.—Psa. 47:7.
I will praise the Lord with my whole heart.—Psa. 111:1.

THEY praise God with half a heart, who either having devotion, want understanding; or else endued with understanding, want devotion.—JOHN BOYS.

The water of saints' praises is drawn out of a deep spring, the heart.—GEORGE SWINNOCK.

Abel's heart was on fire as well as his sacrifice.
—STEPHEN CHARNOCK.

Study your own baseness, if you would be thankful.
—THOMAS GOODWIN.

In holy devotion, first tune well a prepared heart, then sound well a cheerful tongue.—JOHN BOYS.

To bless God for mercies is the way to increase them; to bless him for miseries is the way to remove them.
—WILLIAM DYER.

Those blessings are sweetest that are won with prayers and worn with thanks.—THOMAS GOODWIN.

4 November

THE SOUL AND THE WORLD

For what is a man advantaged, if he gain the whole world, and lose himself, or be cast away?—Luke 9:25.

WHAT profit to win Venice, and then be hanged at the gates thereof?—JOHN TRAPP.

Gain in the chest and loss in the conscience is but a bad exchange.—WILLIAM JENKYN.

He is worthy to die who will lose his soul to save his labour.
—RICHARD ALLEINE.

A prosperous iniquity is the most unprosperous condition of the whole world.—JOHN OWEN.

Rather venture the breaking of the casket than the losing of the jewel.—THOMAS FULLER.

Outward gains are ordinarily attended with inward losses.
—JOHN FLAVEL.

Ahab never bought a dearer purchase than Naboth's vineyard, for which he paid not one penny.—GEORGE SWINNOCK.

5 November

THE DEVIL SELF-DEFEATED

That through death he might destroy him that had the power of death, that is, the devil.—Heb. 2:14.

GOD sets the devil to catch himself.—WILLIAM GURNALL.

The blow which Satan gave our Lord struck himself.
—JEAN DAILLÉ.

The serpent in bruising Christ's heel got a bruise in his own head.—ELISHA COLES.

The devil, by his malice, made Job more famous.
—RICHARD STOCK.

Satan, as in his first temptation, is still on the losing side.
—WILLIAM GURNALL.

God makes the devil a polisher; while he intends to be a destroyer.—STEPHEN CHARNOCK.

Satan got nothing by his winnowing; Peter lost some of his chaff which might well be spared.—ELISHA COLES.

6 November

COVETOUSNESS AND EVIL

The love of money is a root of all kinds of evil.—1 Tim. 6:10. (R.V.)

IT is the *love*, not the *lack* of money, that makes men churls.
—JOHN TRAPP.

Wealth is the devil's stirrup whereby he gets up and rides the covetous.—THOMAS ADAMS.

Many a man's gold hath lost him his God.
—GEORGE SWINNOCK.

The itch of covetousness makes a man scratch what he can from another.—THOMAS WATSON.

Many a Laban is more solicitous of his flock than of his family.
—JOHN TRAPP.

He is too covetous that Jesus Christ cannot satisfy.
—THOMAS ADAMS.

Covetous men, though they have enough to sink them, yet have they never enough to satisfy them.—JOHN TRAPP.

7 November

FAITH, HOPE, AND LOVE

Faith, hope, love, these three.—1 Cor. 13:13. (R.V.)

CHRIST enjoins faith, in saying *Father*; love, in saying *our*; hope in saying *which art in heaven*.—JOHN BOYS.

For hope is ever accompanied with two sisters, which never depart from her sides and society, faith and love.
—JOHN KING.

In his Gospel John teacheth especially faith; in his Epistles, especially love; in his Apocalypse, especially hope.
—JOHN BOYS.

Faith is the mother-grace, for hope is born of her; but charity floweth from them both.—JOHN BUNYAN.

To make in ourselves the building of salvation we need the foundation of faith, the walls of hope, the roof of charity.
—JOHN BOYS.

Faith is the centre and love the circle.—THOMAS ADAMS.

8 November

IDLENESS AND LAZINESS

This was the iniquity ... abundance of idleness.—Ezek. 16:49.
An idle soul shall suffer hunger.—Prov. 19:15.

THE Romans were so idle as to make idleness a god, yet they allowed not that idle idol a temple within the city, but without the walls.—THOMAS ADAMS.

The first-born of idleness is to do nothing.—JOHN KING.

He that plays all summer may dance all winter, but he shall have sorry music to it.—THOMAS ADAMS.

Zeal is out of grace with most men who sit still.
—THOMAS WILSON.

An idle person is poverty's prisoner; if he live without a calling, poverty hath a calling to arrest him.—JOHN BOYS.

Deny sloth not only continuance but countenance.
—THOMAS ADAMS.

They are utterly out that think to have the pleasure of sloth and the guerdon* of goodness.—JOHN TRAPP.

---

* Guerdon = reward.

9 NOVEMBER

KNOWLEDGE WITHOUT OBEDIENCE

*To him that knoweth to do good, and doeth it not,
to him it is sin.*—James 4:17.

TO know good and do ill, makes a man's own mittimus* to hell.—THOMAS ADAMS.

He that dislikes to do what he knows, will one day not know what to do.—WILLIAM SECKER.

Sin in ignorance is a talent of lead, but sin in knowledge is a millstone to sink a man to the lowest.

—THOMAS ADAMS.

We are dull to learn what we should do, and more dull to do what we have learned.—WILLIAM JENKYN.

Judas heard all Christ's sermons.—THOMAS GOODWIN.

The devil knows good, but he is not good.—RICHARD SIBBES.

The devil hath a greater knowledge of God's being than any man upon earth, but since he is a rebel to his will, he is not happy by his knowledge.—STEPHEN CHARNOCK.

---

* Mittimus = a warrant committing a person to prison.

10 November

REPENTANCE—HUMAN AND DIVINE

The Lord will repent.—Jer. 26:13.

Godly sorrow worketh repentance unto salvation, a repentance which bringeth no regret.—2 Cor. 7:10. (R.V.)

THERE cannot be a true sorrow of heart for a sin that is past, but presently there doth arise a purpose not to sin for the future.—THOMAS GOODWIN.

Repentance with man is the changing of his will; repentance with God is the willing of a change.—JOHN TRAPP.

True humiliation is ever joined with reformation.
—RICHARD SIBBES.

Though true repentance is never too late, yet late repentance is seldom true.—THOMAS BROOKS.

When it repenteth a man to have begun well, it is a sinful repentance, and much to be repented of.—JOHN KING.

Let the quantity of thy sins be the measure of thy repentance.
—ISAAC BARGRAVE.

Amendment of life is the best repentance.—JOHN TRAPP.

11 November

THE TIMES AND TODAY

Say not thou, What is the cause that the former days were better than these?—Eccles. 7:10.
Wise men, which knew the times.—Esth. 1:13.
The times that went over him.—1 Chron. 29:30.
The Holy Ghost saith, To day.—Heb. 3:7.

'SAY not thou, that the former days were better than these', but thank God that there is any good in these, bad as they are.—MATTHEW HENRY.

When I consider that our hearts are no softer, I wonder that the times are no harder.—WILLIAM SECKER.

Times are bad, God is good.—RICHARD SIBBES.

If we cannot make the times good, they should not make us bad.—WILLIAM JENKYN.

Today with God is no tomorrow or yesterday.
—THOMAS GOODWIN.

None can be called thy day but this day.—HENRY SMITH.

One today is worth *two* tomorrows.—WILLIAM SECKER.

12 November

INGRATITUDE

A poor wise man, ... by his wisdom delivered the city; yet no man remembered that same poor man.—Eccles. 9:15.
Yet did not the chief butler remember Joseph.—Gen. 40:23.

WHAT the sin against the Holy Ghost is in divinity, that ingratitude is in morality, an offence unpardonable.
—THOMAS FULLER.

Ingratitude is the grave of all God's blessings.—RICHARD SIBBES.

Ingratitude, say some, is a monster in nature, a solecism in manners, and a paradox in grace.—THOMAS BROOKS.

Do an unthankful man nineteen kindnesses, unless you make the twentieth all is lost.—JOHN TRAPP.

He that hath a hand to take, and no tongue to thank, deserves neither hand nor tongue, but to be lame and dumb hereafter.—THOMAS FULLER.

Eaten bread is soon forgotten.—JOHN TRAPP.

Injuries are registered in marble to all posterity, whilst benefits are written on the sand.—THOMAS FULLER.

13 November

PATIENCE

The patient in spirit.—Eccles. 7:8.
A great eagle ... longwinged [lit. *patient-winged*].—Ezek. 17:3.
Patience of hope.—1 Thess. 1:3.

PATIENCE is the life of God's providence in this world.
—HENRY SMITH.

Patience bears all on hope's back.—WILLIAM GURNALL.

Patience is that virtue which had rather suffer evil and do none, than do evil and suffer none.—THOMAS ADAMS.

To lengthen my patience is the best way to shorten my troubles.
—GEORGE SWINNOCK.

Hope is the mother of patience.—WILLIAM JENKYN.

Mercy is one end of patience.—HENRY SMITH.

Seldom is a patient man inquisitive or an inquisitive man patient.—JOHN TRAPP.

14 November

MEDITATION

Meditate upon these things.—1 Tim. 4:15.
Higgaion [margin, *Meditation*]. *Selah* [*A pause*].—Psa. 9:16.

OUR design in meditation must be rather to cleanse our hearts, than to clear our heads.—GEORGE SWINNOCK.

Meditate on our making, that we may fall in love with our Maker.—DAVID DICKSON.

Meditation is the acting of all the powers of the soul.
—RICHARD BAXTER.

Meditation is chewing the cud. Meditation, is the bellows of the affections.—THOMAS WATSON.

Meditation is the life of most other duties.—RICHARD BAXTER.

Meditation applieth, meditation healeth, meditation instructeth.
—EZEKIEL CULVERWELL.

Cogitation provides food, application eats it, resolution digests it.
—GEORGE SWINNOCK.

15 November

THE EVIL OF RICHES

The abundance of the rich will not suffer him to sleep.—Eccles. 5:12.
A grievous evil … riches kept by the owner to his hurt.
—Eccles. 5:13. (R.V.)

MAN may as soon fill a chest with grace, or a vessel with virtue, as a heart with wealth.—THOMAS BROOKS.

Riches and content are like two buckets, while one comes up full, the other goes down empty.—THOMAS ADAMS.

Gold and silver are fitter to set our feet than our hearts upon.
—WILLIAM JENKYN.

In suits both of law and of love, money weighs and sways much.
—JOHN TRAPP.

A shoe may have a silver lace on it, yet pinch the foot.
—THOMAS WATSON.

All the Cains (possessions) of Adam are Abels (vanity).
—GEORGE SWINNOCK.

Earthly riches are full of poverty.—THOMAS BROOKS.

16 November

SPEECH REVEALS MEN

Thy speech betrayeth thee.—Matt. 26:73.
Say now Shibboleth: and he said Sibboleth.—Judg. 12:6.

WE know metals by their tinkling, and men by their talking.
—THOMAS BROOKS.

By the striking of the clapper, we guess at the metal of the bell.
—WILLIAM SECKER.

The word of a man is as powerful as himself.—RICHARD SIBBES.

Good men will be always discovering themselves.
—THOMAS MANTON.

If Christ have his throne upon your conscience, his sceptre will appear upon your conversation.—CHRISTOPHER NESSE.

Words are the looking-glass of the mind.—THOMAS WATSON.

Every man's conversation is suitable to his calling; he whose trade is heavenly follows that close.—WILLIAM GURNALL.

17 November

GOD FORSAKING MEN

He [Samson] wist not that the Lord was departed from him.
—Judg. 16:20.

I let them go after the stubbornness of their heart.—Psa. 81:12. (R.V.)

GOD punishes most when he does not punish.
—THOMAS WATSON.

When the rope is designed, the rod is spared.
—GEORGE SWINNOCK.

If man like not of God's choice, he leaveth them to their own, of which they shall be sure to repent.—RICHARD BERNARD.

Seldom does God suffer men to be their own carvers, but they cut their own fingers.—WILLIAM JENKYN.

There is nothing more to be dreaded than that the Lord should allow us loose reins.—JOHN CALVIN.

When God takes away correction, damnation enters the doors.
—THOMAS ADAMS.

God's leaving one soul to one lust is far worse than leaving him to all the lions in the world.—GEORGE SWINNOCK.

18 November

PLEASURES OF THE WORLD

The delights of the sons of men.—Eccles. 2:8.
Pleasures of this life.—Luke 8:14.

PLEASURES are like the popish relics, the interest is more than the principal.—THOMAS ADAMS.

Worldly comforts are like a narrow tablecloth upon a broad table; those on both sides pull to themselves; and on neither side have they enough.—WILLIAM JENKYN.

The comforts of this life are as candles that will end in a snuff.
—STEPHEN CHARNOCK.

Prisoners' pittance, which neither keeps alive nor suffers to die.
—JOHN TRAPP.

Nothing between two dishes: a splendid service of silver plate, and when you take the cover off there is no food to eat; such are the pleasures here.—GEORGE HERBERT.

The earth is big in our hopes, but little in our hands.
—WILLIAM SECKER.

All earthly things are as salt water, that increases the appetite, but satisfies not.—RICHARD SIBBES.

19 November

FALSEHOOD

Lie not one to another.—Col. 3:9.
A man walking in a spirit of falsehood.—Mic. 2:11. (R.V. Margin.)

A WILFUL falsehood is a cripple and cannot stand alone. It is easy to tell one lie, hard to tell but one lie.
—THOMAS FULLER.

The trade of lying hath crept into all trades.
—GEORGE SWINNOCK.

Some men lie to save their credit; and that is as if one should wipe his mouth on his sleeve to spare his napkin.
—THOMAS ADAMS.

Lying is cousin germane to stealing.—JOHN BOYS.

Hypocrisy is the loudest lie.—GEORGE SWINNOCK.

Till a man be a gracious man, he shall be a double man.
—RICHARD SIBBES.

Perjury is nothing else but a lie bound with an oath.
—JOHN BOYS.

Oftentimes falsehood hath a fairer gloss of probability than truth.—RICHARD SIBBES.

20 November

REPUTATION WITH OR WITHOUT CHARACTER

Honour me now, I pray thee, before the elders of my people.
—1 Sam. 15:30.

HE that desires honour is not worthy of honour.
—WILLIAM SECKER.

When the church of Sardis was really dead, the principal means of keeping it in that condition was the name it had to be alive.—JOHN OWEN.

A good name upon an unchanged nature is but white feathers upon a black skin.—WILLIAM JENKYN.

You say there be more of the company than of the livery; but for heaven and the profession of the gospel, there be more of the livery than be of the company.—THOMAS ADAMS.

Virtue is a thousand escutcheons.*—JOHN TRAPP.

An humble spirit loves a low seat.—WILLIAM GURNALL.

The devil deserves his name.—HENRY SMITH.

---

* Escutcheon = a shield.

21 November

WARNINGS

He heard the sound of the trumpet, and took not warning; his blood shall be upon him.—Ezek. 33:5.
Knowing these things beforehand, beware.—2 Pet. 3:17. (R.V.)

THE axe must first be laid *to* thy root in a way of threatening, before it is laid *at* thy root by way of execution.
—JOHN BUNYAN.

Seest thou another man shipwrecked? Look well to thy tacklings.
—JOHN TRAPP.

Premonition is the best pre-munition.—THOMAS WATSON.

Darts foreseen are dintless.—JOHN TRAPP.

Every man's passing-bell hangs in his own steeple.
—WILLIAM SECKER.

God loves to premonish before he punish.—JOHN TRAPP.

Sickness is but a harbinger to bespeak a lodging for death.
—THOMAS WATSON.

He deserves to break his shins that stumbleth twice at one stone.
—GEORGE SWINNOCK.

22 NOVEMBER

SELF-RIGHTEOUSNESS AND CHRIST'S RIGHTEOUSNESS

Not having mine own righteousness, which is of the law, but that which is through the faith of Christ.—Phil. 3:9.

RIGHTEOUSNESS by works was the first liquor that ever was put into the vessel, and it still retains the tang and savour of it.—JOHN FLAVEL.

The *terminus a quo* is self, the *terminus ad quem** is Christ.
—STEPHEN CHARNOCK.

It is faith alone that will show us the way out of our own doors.
—WILLIAM GURNALL.

A tawny person among negroes thinks himself white.
—JOHN CALVIN.

Men are more unwilling to part with their righteousness than with their sins.—STEPHEN CHARNOCK.

If you be found in your own righteousness you will be lost in your own righteousness.—WILLIAM SECKER.

Peter cannot be justified by the righteousness of Paul; but both may be justified by the righteousness of Christ.
—JOHN FLAVEL.

---

* *Terminus a quo* = starting point; *terminus ad quem* = the point at which something ends or finishes.

23 November

A GOOD HEART

An honest and good heart.—Luke 8:15.
Let my heart be sound.—Psa. 119:80.

A GOOD heart will rather lie in the dust than rise by wickedness.—JOHN TRAPP.

Whoever would have sound happiness must have a sound heart.
—RICHARD GREENHAM.

A gracious heart is like a musical instrument, which, though it be never so exactly tuned, a small matter brings it out of tune again.—JOHN FLAVEL.

The heart is a triangle, which only the Trinity can fill.
—THOMAS WATSON.

A fervent cannot be a vagrant heart.—JOHN FLAVEL.

God alone sees the heart; the heart alone sees God.
—THOMAS MANTON.

Good affections soon kindle in a gracious heart.—JOHN TRAPP.

What cometh from the heart, will go to the heart.
—HENRY WILKINSON.

24 NOVEMBER
WHOLENESS OF BODY AND HOLINESS OF SOUL

Beloved, I wish above all things that thou mayest prosper and be in health, even as thy soul prospereth.—3 John 2.

HOLINESS hath in it a natural tendency to life and peace.
—ELISHA COLES.

Sanctified sickness is far better than unsanctified soundness.
—GEORGE SWINNOCK.

The face is not so deformed that hath lost its eye, as the soul is that loseth its holiness.—WILLIAM GURNALL.

What health is to the heart, that holiness is to the soul.
—JOHN FLAVEL.

A distempered body may have a healthy soul.
—GEORGE SWINNOCK.

The goodness of a saint is not like the redness of blushing but the ruddiness of complexion.—JEAN DAILLÉ.

The soul is the face on which God's image is stamped; holiness is the beauty of this face.—WILLIAM GURNALL.

Integrality is the true note of integrity.—GEORGE SWINNOCK.

25 November

HOPE

God ... hath begotten us again unto a lively hope.—1 Pet. 1:3.
Good hope.—2 Thess. 2:16.
Blessed hope.—Titus 2:13.

A SAD heart does not become a lively hope.
—WILLIAM GURNALL.

The life of our mortal life is the hope of an immortal.
—JEAN DAILLÉ.

Hope can never be put from her holdfast.—JOHN KING.

Nothing more unbecomes an heavenly hope than an earthly heart.—WILLIAM GURNALL.

Better God's heirs live upon hope than upon hire.
—SAMUEL RUTHERFORD.

Weak hope is short-breathed.—WILLIAM GURNALL.

Hope, the sweetest and pleasantest companion that ever travelled with the sojourners upon earth.—JOHN KING.

26 November

THE DANGER OF MERE KNOWLEDGE

Knowledge puffeth up.—1 Cor. 8:1.

THAT knowledge which puffs up will at last puff down.
—JOSEPH CARYL.

He that is proud of his knowledge is a prodigy; for he hath the gout in the wrong end: others have it in their feet, he hath it in his pate.*—THOMAS ADAMS.

Almost all men are infected with the disease of desiring to obtain useless knowledge.—JOHN CALVIN.

Speculative knowledge, like Rachel, is fair but barren.
—WILLIAM GURNALL.

Our hearts are so big (like children that have the rickets) that all the body fares the worse for it.—JOHN TRAPP.

Naked knowledge may make the head giddy, but it will never make the heart holy.—WILLIAM SECKER.

If you know all things, and cannot truly say, 'I know whom I have believed', you have but knowledge enough to know yourselves truly miserable.—JOSEPH HALL.

---

* Pate = head.

27 November

THE LONGSUFFERING OF GOD

The Lord is slow to anger.—Nah. 1:3.
And yet for all that.—Lev. 26:44.

GOD was but six days in making the whole world, yet seven days in destroying one city.—JOHN TRAPP.

Though the patience of God be *lasting*, yet it is not *everlasting*.
—WILLIAM SECKER.

Mercy hath a heaven, and justice a hell, to display itself to eternity, but longsuffering hath only a short-lived earth.
—HENRY SMITH.

Many have been reprieved that were never forgiven.
—STEPHEN CHARNOCK.

God's forbearance is no acquittance.—JOHN TRAPP.

Many will howl when God strikes them and laugh at him when he forbears them.—STEPHEN CHARNOCK.

Because justice seems to wink, men suppose her blind.
—WILLIAM SECKER.

28 November

RELIGION (VAIN)

This man's religion is vain.—James 1:26.

RELIGION hath but loose hold of them that hath no better hold of it.—WILLIAM GURNALL.

Religion must not be in the cockboat,* but in the ship.
—ARCHIBALD CAMPBELL.

He that will not have the *sweat* must not expect the *sweet* of religion.—JOHN FLAVEL.

A pluralist in religion is indeed a neutralist.—THOMAS ADAMS.

Many will walk with religion when she wears her silver slippers.
—JOHN BUNYAN.

The sweet bait of religion hath drawn many to nibble at it, who are offended with the hard service it calls to.
—WILLIAM GURNALL.

If the world get the start of religion in the morning, it will be hard for religion to overtake it all the day after.
—JOHN FLAVEL.

Jehu only made religion a stirrup to mount upon the saddle of popularity.—WILLIAM SECKER.

* Cockboat = a small boat towed behind a larger vessel.

29 November

HEART AND HEAD

The whole head ... and the whole heart.—Isa. 1:5.

A HEART full of graces is better than a head full of notions.
—THOMAS GOODWIN.

If the mind be not stirring, the affections will be nodding.
—GEORGE SWINNOCK.

Light can make a good head, only heat can make a good heart.
—WILLIAM JENKYN.

Many a one is now in hell that had a better head than thine; and many a one now in heaven that complained of as bad a heart as thine.—JOHN FLAVEL.

What is a knowing head without a fruitful heart?
—THOMAS WATSON.

An erroneous head and a godly heart will not meet.
—WILLIAM JENKYN.

A sanctified heart is better than a silver tongue.
—THOMAS GOODWIN.

First have a new heart, and then you cannot want a new tongue.
—CHRISTOPHER NESSE.

30 November

SUBMISSION

There went out fire from the Lord, and devoured them [Aaron's sons] … and Aaron held his peace.—Lev. 10:2, 3.

WE must lay our hands upon our mouths when God's hand is upon our backs.—JOHN TRAPP.

There is no way to avoid perishing by Christ's iron rod, but by kissing his golden sceptre.—THOMAS BROOKS.

It is the surest and shortest way to get our will, in so far as may be for our well, to allow him to take his own way and will with us.—JOSEPH CHURCH.

Jonah shuts up his prophecy, and lets God have the last word.
—JOHN TRAPP.

A woolpack* doth conquer the strength of an ordnance† by yielding unto it.—THOMAS FULLER.

None so mighty that is greater or so mean that is less, than a subject to God and his ordinances.—JOHN BOYS.

The less any man strives for himself, the more is God his champion.—JOHN TRAPP.

---

* Woolpack = a sack full of wool.
† Ordnance = cannon ball.

1 December

LOVE OF THE WORLD

Love not the world, neither the things that are in the, world ... the world passeth away, and the lust thereof.—1 John 2:15, 17.

THE Christian descends far below his quality, when he is much taken with anything in this place of his exile.
—ARCHBISHOP LEIGHTON.

Love not the world, for that is a moth in a Christian's life.
—JOHN BUNYAN.

A godly man preferreth grace before goods, and wisdom before the world.—RICHARD BERNARD.

Divorce the flesh from the world, and then the devil can do us no harm.—JOHN TRAPP.

He that despiseth not earth was never yet inwardly called to heaven.—THOMAS ADAMS.

Mortality is the disgrace of all sublunary delights.
—RICHARD BAXTER.

They who love the world most leave it worst.
—GEORGE SWINNOCK.

There is no greater danger in the world than to live in danger of the world.—THOMAS ADAMS.

2 December

HUMAN FRAILTY AND GOD'S TREASURE

We have this treasure in earthen vessels, that the excellency of the power may be of God, and not of us.—2 Cor. 4:7.

MINISTERS are but Gideon's pitchers, with the light of the gospel in them.—RICHARD SIBBES.

The treasure of life is deposited in a brittle vessel.
—STEPHEN CHARNOCK.

It is better to be a wooden vessel filled with wine, than a golden one filled with water.—WILLIAM SECKER.

God's choice acquaintances are humble men.
—ROBERT LEIGHTON.

Ministers are but the pole; it is to the brazen serpent you are to look.—STEPHEN CHARNOCK.

God can put a golden bias into a leaden bowl.
—WILLIAM SECKER.

We should have mean thoughts of the nothingness of our reason when we consider the sublimity of the divine wisdom.
—STEPHEN CHARNOCK.

3 December

SERMONS

That which we have seen and heard declare we unto you.—1 John 1:3.
We also believe, and therefore speak.—2 Cor. 4:13.

A SERMON is not made with an eye upon the sermon, but with both eyes upon the people and all the heart upon God.
—JOHN OWEN

No man preaches that sermon well to others, who doth not first preach it to his own heart.—JOHN OWEN.

As every sound is not music, so every sermon is not preaching.
—HENRY SMITH.

That is the best sermon that is digged out of a man's own breast.
—JOHN TRAPP.

Every good sermon hath in it two things, a bridle and a spur; to meet with two dispositions in men, inclination to evil, aversement from good. For the former precipice there is a bridle; for the latter dulness a spur; these must be strained, those restrained.—THOMAS ADAMS.

God chose those to preach mercy who had felt most mercy.
—RICHARD SIBBES.

4 December

HOUSE AND HOME

And every man went unto his own house.—John 7:53.
The disciples went away again unto their own home.—John 20:10.

WHAT need they travel far whose felicity is at home?
—THOMAS ADAMS.

Lazarus was happy when *sine domo*, because he was not *sine Domino*.*—GEORGE SWINNOCK.

You are everywhere at home, but there where you are strangers to God.—THOMAS MANTON.

A poor man in his house is like a snail in his shell; crush that and you will kill him.—JOHN TRAPP.

Neglect of family prayer, as it were, uncovers the roofs of men's houses, and makes for a curse to be rained down on their table.—THOMAS WATSON.

The prodigal changed many places ere he came home.
—JOHN TRAPP.

A thread is enough to hale† one home.—DAVID DICKSON.

---

* *Sine domo* = without a home; *sine Domino* = without a Lord.
† Hale = drag.

5 December

LUXURY

That lie upon beds of ivory, and abound with superfluities.
—Amos 6:4. (Margin.)

THE right way to put out the fire of lust is to withdraw the fuel of excess.—WILLIAM JENKYN.

Pomp and prosperity, then, is no sure note of the true church.
—JOHN TRAPP.

Christ did not die to purchase this world for us.
—THOMAS ADAMS.

Any good will serve the turn of those who know not the *chief good*.—WILLIAM SECKER.

Ahab hath an ivory house; the godly wander in dens and caves of the earth.—THOMAS FULLER.

Either Peter and Paul were fools who lived so poorly, or their successors are to blame that live so pompously.
—JOHN TRAPP.

To rot and to riot differ but one small letter.
—THOMAS ADAMS.

6 December

SOUL AND SPIRIT

Your spirit and soul.—1 Thess. 5:23. (R.V.)

SOUL is that by which we live naturally; spirit is that by which we live through grace supernaturally.—JOHN BOYS.

Souls have no sexes.—GEORGE SWINNOCK.

The soul of the soul is perception.—JOHN CALVIN.

As God's eternal decrees have an end without a beginning, so the souls of men have a beginning without an end.
—JOHN BOYS.

Our souls are like the mill that grinds what is put into it.
—RICHARD SIBBES.

Fill thy spirit with spirituals and thy soul with the honour of God.—SIR THOMAS BROWNE.

7 December

THE GODLY AND THE UNGODLY

The Lord doth put a difference between the Egyptians and Israel.
—Exod. 11:7.

THERE is a wide difference between a child under wrath and a child of wrath.—THOMAS GOODWIN.

As the wicked are hurt by the best things, so the godly are bettered by the worst.—WILLIAM JENKYN.

The wicked in the fulness of their sufficiency are in straits (Job 20:22), while the godly in the fulness of their straits are in a sufficiency.—JOHN TRAPP.

It is an evil man's cross ... and a good man's joy to be kept back from sin.—OBADIAH SEDGWICK.

God cannot endure that in his fields which he suffers in the wilderness.—JOHN FLAVEL.

A sinner falls into sin as a fish, the saint as a child does into the water. In the latter sin is, but the former is in sin.
—WILLIAM JENKYN.

8 December

NEGLIGENCE

My sons, be not now negligent.—2 Chron. 29:11.

ALL negligence in good things is from the want of love.
—THOMAS ADAMS.

It is bad to neglect our duty, but it is worse to vouch providence for the patronizing of our neglects.—MATTHEW HENRY.

He that is far from his business is not far from loss.
—JOHN TRAPP.

A competent estate well husbanded is better than a vast patrimony neglected.—THOMAS ADAMS.

Idleness is the burial of our persons, and negligence is the burial of our actions.—GEORGE SWINNOCK.

Many a man hath been thrown out of the saddle of profession by riding with too slack a rein of circumspection.
—WILLIAM SECKER.

The common ass was never well saddled.—THOMAS ADAMS.

You must not be diligent in one relation and negligent in another.—CHRISTOPHER NESSE.

9 December

WARNING AGAINST EVIL COMPANIONSHIP

*O my soul, come not thou into their secret;
unto their assembly, mine honour, be not thou united.*—Gen. 49:6.

IF you love near relations to wicked men, Christ will have no relation to you.—DAVID DICKSON.

Division is better than agreement in evil.—GEORGE HUTCHESON.

In this fellowship, riot is the host, drunkenness the guest, swearing keeps the reckoning, lust holds the door, and beggary pays the shot.—THOMAS ADAMS.

Unity without verity is no better than conspiracy.
—JOHN TRAPP.

Yoke-fellows in sin are yoke-fellows in pain; the soul is punished for informing, the body for performing.—JOHN DONNE.

That match may be lawfully broken off, which was first most unlawfully made.—THOMAS FULLER.

Verity consisteth not in the plurality of voices.
—THOMAS FULLER.

10 December

PERSECUTORS

Her persecutors overtook her between the straits.—Lam. 1:3.

THERE will always be Cains to persecute Abels.
—JOHN TRAPP.

Herodias had rather have the blood of a saint than half a kingdom.—LEWIS STUCKLEY.

While there is a devil and a wicked man in the world, never expect a charter of exemption from trouble.
—THOMAS WATSON.

Once tyrants cannot prevail with craft, they come to cruelty; when politicians' rhetoric fails, Carters' logic* must do the feat.—JOHN BOYS.

Paul well joins persecution and a Pharisee together, for there was never hypocrite but he was a persecutor.
—RICHARD SIBBES.

When the rod hath done its office then it is thrown into the fire.—ZEPHANIAH SMYTH.

In spite of all devils there shall be saints.—JOSEPH HALL.

---

* Carter's logic = i.e. the use of the whip.

11 December

HEAVEN

Thy holy habitation ... heaven.—Deut. 26:15.
His holy heaven.—Psa. 20:6.
Whither the tribes go up.—Psa. 122:4.
They desire a better country.—Heb. 11:16.

WHEREVER thou meetest a Christian, he is going to heaven.—WILLIAM GURNALL.

Worldly things are but a tabernacle, a movable; heaven is a mansion: whatsoever become of the former, if thou canst keep the other, say, 'I have lost that I could not keep, I have kept that I cannot lose.'—THOMAS ADAMS.

Heaven is not a lease which soon expires, but an inheritance.
—THOMAS WATSON.

Heaven will pay for the loss of anything that we can lose to get it, but nothing can pay for the loss of heaven.
—RICHARD BAXTER.

In heaven is no *warfare*, but all *welfare*.—JOHN BOYS.

Heaven is reserved for heaven.—JAMES JANEWAY.

Heaven is the proper place for comfort, earth for grace.
—GEORGE SWINNOCK.

12 December

TROUBLES—MANY AND VARIOUS

My brethren, count it all joy when ye fall into divers temptations.
—James 1:2.

Many are the afflictions of the righteous.—Psa. 34:19.

CROSSES seldom come single.—THOMAS MANTON.

We may sin in being overmuch troubled at things for which it is a sin not to be troubled.—RICHARD SIBBES.

Life and trouble are married together.—THOMAS WATSON.

Affliction is a pill, which, being wrapped up in patience and quiet submission, may be easily swallowed; but discontent chews the pill and embitters the soul.—JOHN FLAVEL.

Sufferings are but as little chips of the cross.—JOSEPH CHURCH.

Divers diseases must have divers remedies. Pride, envy, covetousness, worldliness, ambition are not all cured by the same physic.*—THOMAS MANTON.

---

* Physic = medicine.

13 December

HOLINESS

The beauties of holiness.—Psa. 110:3.
The way of holiness.—Isa. 35:8.
The spirit of holiness. Rom. 1:4.

THERE is a beauty in holiness as well as a beauty of holiness.—GEORGE SWINNOCK.

Holiness is a constellation of graces.—THOMAS BOSTON.

Holiness is the symmetry of the soul.—MATTHEW HENRY.

Sow holiness and reap happiness.—GEORGE SWINNOCK.

Holiness is our doormark, and our forehead mark, the destroying angel shall pass over.—EDWARD MARBURY.

Holiness is right nobility.—THOMAS ADAMS.

Holiness and charity are like father and child.
—GEORGE SWINNOCK.

14 December
THE FALL (CONSEQUENCES OF)

Judgment was by one to condemnation.—Rom. 5:16.
In Adam all die.—1 Cor. 15:22.

MAN, by his fall, wounded his head and heart; the wound in the head made him unstable in the truth, and that in his heart unsteadfast in his affections.—STEPHEN CHARNOCK.

Sin has turned the world from a paradise into a thicket, there is no getting through without being scratched.
—THOMAS BOSTON.

The aspiring thoughts of the first man run in the veins of his posterity.—STEPHEN CHARNOCK.

Since the tree of knowledge hath been tasted, the key of knowledge hath been rusted.—WILLIAM SECKER.

In the first man, the person corrupted the nature; in every other man nature corrupts the person.—WILLIAM JENKYN.

When man proved unfaithful to God his maker, the earth proved unfruitful to man her manurer.—THOMAS FULLER.

15 December

OBEDIENCE

Now therefore hearken, O Israel, unto the statutes and unto the judgments, which I teach you, for to do them.—Deut. 4:1.

Not a hearer that forgetteth, but a doer that worketh.
—James 1:25. (R.V.)

THIS is the true obedience, whether to God or man, when we look not so much to the letter of the law, as to the mind of the law-maker.—JOHN TRAPP.

In all true obedience there is remembrance.—WILLIAM JENKYN.

The root is faith, the sap is fear, the fruit is obedience.
—RICHARD SIBBES.

The best almanac we can rely upon for seasonable weather and the lengthening of our tranquillity is our obedience to God.—JOHN TRAPP.

It is our bounden duty to live *in* obedience, but it would prove our utter ruin to live *on* obedience.—WILLIAM SECKER.

He doth not his master's but his own will, that doth no more than himself will.—JOHN TRAPP.

16 December

HEAVEN AND HOLINESS

Holiness, without which no man shall see the Lord.—Heb. 12:14.

IF you would be better satisfied what the beautiful vision means, my request is that you would live holily and go and see.—JOHN BUNYAN.

Heaven is large but the way to heaven must be narrow.
—HENRY SMITH.

Glory is disclosed from no other bud but holiness.
—JOHN FLAVEL.

Holiness is that perspective through which we must see God.
—THOMAS ADAMS.

The new man is the only citizen of the new Jerusalem.
—GEORGE SWINNOCK.

The saints are most heavenly when nearest to heaven; like as rivers, the nearer they grow to the sea, the sooner they are met by the tide.—JOHN TRAPP.

Holiness in the seed shall have happiness in the harvest.
—THOMAS ADAMS.

17 December

MEMORY

Keep in memory what I preached unto you.—1 Cor. 15:2.
Forget not all his benefits.—Psa. 103:2.

OUR memory, like jet,* good only to draw straws and treasure up trifles of no moment.

—THOMAS FULLER.

The most precious truths laid up in our memories are jewels put into a crazy cabinet.—WILLIAM JENKYN.

Grace makes a heart-memory, even where there is no good head-memory.—THOMAS BOSTON.

Be careful to keep the old receipts which thou hast from God for the pardon of thy sins.—WILLIAM GURNALL.

Much good comfort is lost for want of memory.

—THOMAS ADAMS.

A shallow understanding causeth a short memory.

—NATHANIEL HOMES.

Memory, the muniment-house† of the soul.

—THOMAS FULLER.

---

* Jet = a type of lignite; once thought to be able to attract straw to itself.
† Muniment-house = a building used for keeping important documents, etc.

18 December

THE HYPOCRITICAL CRITIC

Thou hypocrite, first cast out the beam out of thine own eye; and then shalt thou see clearly to cast out the mote out of thy brother's eye.
—Matt. 7:5.

OUR minds are as ill-set as our eyes – neither of them apt to turn inwards.—JOHN TRAPP.

The watchful cock, first claps his wings to awaken himself, before he crows to awake others.—NEHEMIAH ROGERS.

A blurred finger is unfit to wipe away a blot.—JEAN DAILLÉ.

A cracked bell is not good to call men together, nor is a minister of cracked reputation fit to persuade others to holiness.
—WILLIAM JENKYN.

Many are like barbers, that trim all men but themselves.
—THOMAS ADAMS.

We must not break our neighbour's head with the Pharisee, but smite our own breast with the publican.—JOHN BOYS.

The eye both seeth and correcteth all other things save itself.
—NEHEMIAH ROGERS.

19 December

IDOLATRY

Thou shalt not make unto thee any graven image ... Thou shalt not bow down thyself to them.—Exod. 20:4, 5.

AN image-lover is a God-hater.—THOMAS WATSON.

Blessed is the soul, that, like Jacob's house, hath no idol in it.—JOHN TRAPP.

Idolaters are of a murderous disposition, as their god-devil is whom they worship.—RICHARD BERNARD.

To liken God to any is the grossest idolatry and to liken any to God is the highest arrogance.—GEORGE SWINNOCK.

We are all born idolaters.—THOMAS ADAMS.

The whole stock of images is but a lie of God.
—STEPHEN CHARNOCK.

To pray to saints is idolatry advanced to blasphemy.
—THOMAS WATSON.

Anything above God is idolatry.—RICHARD SIBBES.

20 December

THE HOUSE OF GOD

And he was afraid, and said, How dreadful is this place! this is none other but the house of God.—Gen. 28:17.

THE temple should be the centre of thy circumference.
—NEHEMIAH ROGERS.

Outward decency in the church is an harbinger to provide a lodging for inward devotion.—THOMAS FULLER.

We read not that Christ ever exercised force but once, and that was to drive profane ones out of his temple, not to force them in.—JOHN MILTON.

Many crowd to get into the church, but make no room for the sermon to get into them.—THOMAS ADAMS.

Christ is the way into, but sin is the way out of the temple of God.—JOHN BUNYAN.

God prefers the gates of Zion; not only before one or some, but before all the dwellings of Jacob; and men prefer one such dwelling before the gates of Zion.—DAVID CLARKSON.

The devil was never a friend to temple work.
—WILLIAM GURNALL.

21 December

PLEASURES AND SECURITY

Thou that art given to pleasures, that sittest securely.
—Isa. 47:8. (R.V. Margin.)

SOFT pleasures harden the heart.—THOMAS WATSON.

God often cures a lethargy of security by a fever of perplexity.
—JOHN TRAPP.

Dives and his dishes, Balaam and his wages, Achan and his wedges, Herod and his Herodias, are not easily separated.
—GEORGE SWINNOCK.

A little pleasure for much repentance is but a hard pennyworth.
—THOMAS ADAMS.

We commonly most forget God and ourselves when he remembers us most.—WILLIAM JENKYN.

He purchaseth his pleasure at too dear a rate, that pays his honesty to get it.—JOHN TRAPP.

They are in a deep of security who are never sensible of a deep of sin.—JOHN OWEN.

22 December

HUMAN FRAILTY

All are of the dust, and all turn to dust again.—Eccles. 3:20.

MAN was made of earth which was made of nothing.
—EDWARD MARBURY.

Naturally we tend to nothing as we came from nothing.
—STEPHEN CHARNOCK.

Frailty is a flaw in the best diamond of nature, which abateth its price.—GEORGE SWINNOCK.

The bonds of mortality are so much the stronger by being weaker.—JEAN DAILLÉ.

Rachel ended her journey to heaven in the midst of her journey on earth.—THOMAS FULLER.

Every imperfection is a want of some degree of being.
—STEPHEN CHARNOCK.

The common hope is ill-bottomed.[*]—JOHN TRAPP.

---

[*] Ill-bottomed = rests on a bad foundation.

23 December

THE TONGUE

Set a watch, O Lord, before my mouth; keep the door of my lips.
—Psa. 141:3.

IF we desire to be doorkeepers in God's house, let us entreat God first to be a doorkeeper in our house.—JOHN BOYS.

The heart is the vessel of poisonous liquor, the tongue is but the tap to broach it.—GEORGE SWINNOCK.

Man's mouth, though it be but a little hole, will hold a world full of sin.—EDWARD REYNER.

The key of the mouth ought not to stand in the door of the lips, but to be kept in the cabinet of the mind.—JOHN BOYS.

He may not be accounted an honest man of life that is an evil man in tongue.—NICHOLAS BYFIELD.

The heart is the metal of the bell, the tongue but the clapper.
—GEORGE SWINNOCK.

As man is a little world in the great, so the tongue a great world in the little.—JOHN BOYS.

24 December

MEN, GOOD AND BAD

Discern between good and bad.—1 Kings 3:9.
As many as they found, both bad and good.—Matt. 22:10.

NO man so good, as for all things to be beloved; no man so bad as for anything but sin to be hated.—WILLIAM JENKYN.

The good man is free, though he serves; the evil is bound, though he reigns.—THOMAS ADAMS.

The wheat and the chaff may grow together, but they shall not always lie together.—WILLIAM SECKER.

It is by no means remarkable that the barking of the dogs should annoy the wolves.—JEAN DAILLÉ.

The trees of righteousness are thinly planted in the world's orchard.—WILLIAM SECKER.

The chaff and wheat grow together in the same field, and upon the same root and stalk.—JOHN FLAVEL.

There are many birds of *prey* to one bird of *paradise*.
—WILLIAM SECKER.

25 December

CHRIST'S POVERTY AND OURS

Though he was rich, yet for your sakes he became poor, that ye through his poverty might be rich.—2 Cor. 8:9.

CHRIST'S poverty is our patrimony.—WILLIAM JENKYN.

Christ's poverty was so great, that he was born in another man's house, and buried in another man's tomb.
—JOHN BOYS.

We are so far from paying the uttermost farthing, that at the utmost we have not a farthing to pay.—WILLIAM SECKER.

In his [Christ's] right the world is ours, whatever pittance we enjoy in our own.—JOSEPH HALL.

It is only the prisoner who lives in such a tenement that he may be sure none will seek to take it from him.
—THOMAS WATSON.

The great Architect of the world had not a house to put his head in.—CHRISTOPHER NESSE.

Every Lazarus is not carried into Abraham's bosom.
—THOMAS MANTON.

26 December

HUMILITY AND PRIDE

Every one that is proud in heart is an abomination to the Lord.
—Prov. 16:5.

He shall save the humble person.—Job 22:29.

PRIDE is a sinner's torment, but humility is a saint's ornament.—WILLIAM SECKER.

A humble sinner is in a better condition than a proud angel.
—THOMAS WATSON.

A humble man hath this advantage of a proud man, for he cannot fall.—EDWARD MARBURY.

It is safer to be humble with one talent, than proud with ten; yea, better be a humble worm than a proud angel.
—WILLIAM JENKYN.

Humility is the repentance of pride.—NEHEMIAH ROGERS.

How easy it is to reason out man's humility, but how hard it is to reason man into it.—STEPHEN CHARNOCK.

Humility is the ornament of angels and pride the deformity of devils.—WILLIAM JENKYN.

27 December
HUSBANDS AND WIVES

Husbands, love your wives.—Eph. 5:25.
Wives, submit yourselves unto your own husbands.—Col. 3:18.

THE man and wife are partners, like two oars in a boat.
—HENRY SMITH.

A prudent wife commands her husband by obeying him.
—JOHN TRAPP.

An obedient wife is the likeliest woman in the world to command her husband.—GEORGE SWINNOCK.

Some choose their wives as our grandmother Eve did the apple, because they are pleasant to the eyes to be looked upon.
—THOMAS FULLER.

He that cannot reform his wife without beating, is worthy to be beaten for choosing no better.—HENRY SMITH.

A gracious wife satisfieth a good husband, and silenceth a bad one.—GEORGE SWINNOCK.

The man misseth his rib; the woman would be in her old place again, under the man's arm.—JOHN TRAPP.

28 December

MEDITATION AND PRAYER

Isaac went out to meditate [Margin, *to pray*] *in the field at eventide.*
—Gen. 24:63.

While I was musing the fire burned: then spake I.—Psa. 39:3.

MEDITATION is like the charging of a piece,[*] and prayer the discharging of it.—GEORGE SWINNOCK.

In prayer our meditation is illuminated, and by mediation our devotion in praying inflamed.—JOHN BOYS.

Faith hath wings, and meditation is its chariot.
—RICHARD BAXTER.

Meditation is the best beginning of prayer, and prayer is the best conclusion of meditation.—GEORGE SWINNOCK.

Meditation fills the soul with good liquor, and then prayer broaches it and sets it running.—GEORGE SWINNOCK.

Meditation on our sins helpeth in confession, meditation on our wants helpeth in petition, meditation on our mercies helpeth in thanksgiving.—GEORGE SWINNOCK.

---

[*] Piece = gun.

29 December

THE PHARISEE

One of the Pharisees.—Luke 7:36.

THE Pharisees had many prayers, but never the fewer sins.
—THOMAS ADAMS.

The Pharisees had heaven commonly at their tongue-ends, but the earth continually at their finger-ends.—JOHN TRAPP.

The Pharisees wanted powder to their shot.
—EDWARD MARBURY.

The holiness of the most is not to be as bad as the worst.
—WILLIAM JENKYN.

The Pharisee took thanks to himself in thankfulness to God.
—THOMAS GOODWIN.

Of all devils, none so bad as the professing devil, the preaching, praying devil.—WILLIAM GURNALL.

If God hath made us men, let us not make ourselves gods.
—RICHARD SIBBES.

The Pharisee is no fit husbandman to plough up the Pharisee.
—THOMAS ADAMS.

He that hath a false end in his profession will soon come to the end of it.—WILLIAM GURNALL.

30 December

KEEPING THE WHOLE LAW

Whosoever shall keep the whole law, and yet offend in one point, he is guilty of all.—James 2:10.

MAN may violate *totam legem*, though not *totum legis*.*
—THOMAS MANTON.

Unbelief is radically† all other disobedience.
—ROBERT LEIGHTON.

Where the hedge is lowest man goes over fastest.
—JOSEPH CARYL.

The law of God will not take ninety-nine for a hundred.
—WILLIAM SECKER.

There is a due in a penny, as well as in a pound.
—RICHARD SIBBES.

Partial obedience is an argument of insincerity.
—THOMAS MANTON.

He that does not preserve the law does not observe it.
—WILLIAM JENKYN.

---

* That is, a man may sin against the dignity and authority of *the whole law*, though he does not actually break *every part of the law*.

† Radically = at the root of.

31 December

FINAL PERSEVERANCE

My sheep ... shall never perish,
neither shall any man pluck them out of my hand.—John 10:27, 28.

THOUGH Christians be not kept altogether from falling, yet they are kept from falling altogether.—WILLIAM SECKER.

If one justified person may fall away from Christ all may; and so Christ would be a head without a body.—THOMAS WATSON.

If it be the honour of God to snatch souls out of the devil's hands, it is for his honour to keep them.

—STEPHEN CHARNOCK.

Perseverance (that golden clasp) which joins grace and glory together.—THOMAS FULLER.

Paul, who turned the world upside down, could not be turned upside down by the world.—WILLIAM SECKER.

God's love ties the marriage-knot so fast, that neither death nor hell can break it asunder.—THOMAS WATSON.

Where there is no confidence *in* God, there will be no continuance *with* God.—WILLIAM SECKER.

LIST OF AUTHORS

ADAMS, Thomas
ALLEINE, Joseph
ALLEINE, Richard
ANDREWS, Lancelot
ANNESLEY, Samuel
ASH, Simeon
AUGUSTINE
AUSTIN, William

BAKER, Sir Richard
BARGRAVE, Isaac
BATES, William
BAXTER, Richard
BERNARD, Richard
BEVERIDGE, William
BOSTON, Thomas
BOYS, John
BROOKS, Thomas
BROWN, John
BROWN, Sir Thomas
BUNYAN, John
BURROUGHS, Jeremiah
BYFIELD, Nicholas
CALAMY, Edmund

CALVIN, John
CAMPBELL, Archibald
CARMICHAEL, Alexander
CARYL, Joseph
CAWDRAY, Robert
CHARNOCK, Stephen
CHURCH, Joseph
CLARKSO, David
CLERKE, Richard
COLES, Elisha
COWPER, William
CRADOCK, Walter
CROMWELL, Oliver
CRUSO, Timothy
CULVERWELL, Ezekiel

DAILLÉ, Jean
DICKSON, David
DOD, John
DONNE, John
DOWNAME, George
DURANT, John
DURHAM, James
DYER, William

ESTEY, George

FENNER, William
FLAVEL, John
FULLER, Thomas

GATAKER, Thomas
GOODWIN, Thomas
GRANGER, Thomas
GREENHAM, Richard
GREENHILL, William
GROSSE, Alexander
GURNALL, William

HALL, Joseph
HALL, Thomas
HARDY, Nathaniel
HENRY, Matthew
HENRY, Philip
HERBERT, George
HOMES, Nathaniel
HOOKER, Thomas
HORTON, Thomas
HOWE, John
HUME, John
HUTCHESON, George

JACOMB, Thomas
JANEWAY, James
JENKYN, William

KEACH, Benjamin
KING, John

LEIGHTON, Robert
LUTHER, Martin
LYE, Thomas

MANTON, Thomas
MARBURY, Edward
MILTON, John
MOSSOM, Robert

NESSE, Christopher

OWEN, John

PENDEN, Alexander
POOLE, Matthew

RAINOLDS, John
RANEW, Nathaniel
RAWORTH, Francis
REYNER, Edward
ROGERS, John
ROGERS, Nehemiah
RUTHERFORD, Samuel

SECKER, William
SEDGWICK, Obadiah
SIBBES, Richard

SMITH, Henry
SMYTH, Zephaniah
STOCK, Richard
STRONG, William
STUCKLEY, Lewis
SWINNOCK, George
SYMSON, Archibald

TAYLOR, Jeremy
TAYLOR, Thomas
TRAPP, John

TREFFREY, Richard Junr.

VENNING, Ralph

WATSON, Thomas
WILKINSON, Henry
WILLAN, Edward
WILLETT, Andrew
WILLIAMS, Griffith
WILSON, Thomas
WRIGHT, Abraham

INDEX OF SCRIPTURE TEXTS

CH.	VERSE	PAGE
Genesis		
1:	16	99
3:	6	116
		161
	10	245
	17	306
	21	252
6:	9	98
17:	1	255
18:	19	282
19:	16	214
24:	63	363
28:	17	355
30:	27	23
32:	10	96
	26	172
40:	23	317
47:	9	268
49:	6	249
		344
Exodus		
7:	19	60
9:	20	91
9:	27	234
11:	7	342
20:	4	354
	9, 10	191
23:	1	285
	33	247
32:	24	89
37:	23	108
40:	8	305
Leviticus		
5:	5	234
6:	4	245
10:	2, 3	335
16:	21	112
		128
25:	37	215
26:	10	122
	44	332
Numbers		
15:	30	53
16:	29	147
22:	34	234

23:	7, 10	21	16:	21	84
25:	11	14			

Deuteronomy

Ruth

2:	17	204

1:	17	196
	43	266
4:	1	350
5:	27	175
7:	7, 8	176
26:	15	346
29:	29	167
32:	2	32
33:	21	34

1 Samuel

2:	16	155
13:	12	66
15:	21	66
	24	183
		234
	30	325
16:	7	97
20:	8	155
25:	17	254
26:	21	303
31:	4	15

Joshua

7:	20	234
	21	116

Judges

2 Samuel

1:	7	283
4:	8	155
7:	17	50
8:	1	137
9:	54	134
10:	16	263
11:	39	31
12:	6	321
14:	3	165
16:	16, 17	25
	20	322

6:	16	193
7:	28	274
11:	1, 2	218
12:	5	270
17:	2	229
	23	15

1 Kings

1:	5	45
3:	9	359
8:	18	9

16:	19	120	15:	22	349

1 Corinthians

2 Corinthians

2:	4	79	1:	12	239
	13	210		20	264
	14	275	2:	17	272
	17	79	4:	4	130
5:	8	104		7	337
	11	117		13	338
6:	11	103		17	27
7:	28	159		18	7
	31	201	6:	12	22
	35	87	7:	10	315
8:	1	331	8:	9	360
9:	25	144		12	9
11:	2	231		14	60
	3	77	9:	11	111
		231	10:	10	193
	185		11:	2	286
	16	31		14	297
	28	223	13:	5	223
	30	229			

Galatians

12:	1	210			
	6	156	2:	2	134
	28	69		4	91
	31	235		17	33
13:	13	312	4:	2	139
15:	2	352	5:	13	288
	10	73		17	54
		168			80

6:	10	112	1:	10	272
	14	10		21	132
	16	162	3	8	163
				9	327
				17	40
			4:	22	91

Ephesians

1:	6	219
	12	186
	23	156
2:	3	73
4:	11	69
	12	260
	14	133
	18	209
	22	275
	26	48
5:	4	92
	15	144
	16	301
	18	78
	20	19
	25	362
	26	181
6:	1	282
	5	139
	11	297
	13	101
	18	70

Colossians

1:	18	1
2:	2	170
	18	30
3:	2	22
	9	324
	15	19
	18	362
	23	295
4:	5	112
	14	88
	17	260

1 Thessalonians

1:	3	318
2:	5	157
5:	18	19
	23	341

2 Thessalonians

1:	12	219
2:	3	57
3:	11	123

Philippians

1:	7	67

INDEX OF SCRIPTURE TEXTS

1 Timothy

1:	5	289
	11	213
	14	75
2:	7	75
	9	265
	15	75
4:	2	39
	6	64
	12	241
	13	192
	15	319
5:	20	216
6:	10	311
	18	202
	20	87

2 Timothy

1:	11	64
2:	26	59
3:	2	28, 151
	4	28
	12	8
	15	94
4:	5	69
	6	225
	10	136

Titus

1:	16	158
2:	6	49
	8	180
	13	330
3:	3	104
	5	208
	13	88

Philemon

	8	128
	14	295

Hebrews

2:	14	310
	15	132
3:	7	316
	12	189
6:	1	24
	11	170
	12	75
8:	2	64
9:	1	121
10:	22	17
		39
	25	292
11:	1	17
	6	131
		255
	7	221
	10	106
	16	346

383

11:	26	197	2:	9	186
12:	7, 8	58		14	231
	11	114		16	288
	14	351	4:	13	27
	17	4		15	123
13:	5	198	5:	5	145
	300			8	138
	16	202			

2 Peter

James

1:	2	347	1:	1	278
	3	212		4	226
	15	18	2:	1	269
	25	350		4	113
	26	333		10	249
	27	294		14	244
2:	10	365		22	296
	17	90	3:	5	209
	18	302		16	203
4:	8	98		17	326
	17	314		18	168
5:	15	205			
	16	262			

1 John

1 Peter

1:	3	330	1:	3	338
	7	212		5	51
	21	52	2:	15	336
	23	181		16	201
2:	7	163		17	336
				19	136
				22	297
				26	79

3:	6	86	**Jude**		
	18	267		4	53
4:	6	13		11	244
	8	51		22	108
	17	242	**Revelation**		
			Title:		88
2 John			6:	9	12
	12	192	10:	5, 6	237
			13:	16	99
			14:	6	42
3 John			18:	7	53
	2	329	21:	8	183
	9	43		27	63
	13	150	22:	17	184

INDEX OF SUBJECTS

Accountability, 3
Adversary, 138
Adversity, 293
Affections, 22
Affliction, 20, 27
Ambition, 43
Amen, end
Anger, 48
Answers, 248
Antiquity, 35
Apostacy, 57
Apostates, 136
Apostles, 69
Appearances, 97
Armour, 101
Assurance, 17, 170
Atheism, 118
Atonement, 129
Attention, 85
Attributes of God, 186

Backsliding, 110
Beds, 143
Blindness, 84

Body and soul, 72, 329
Brevity, 237
Business, 220
Busybodies, 123

Captives, 59
Cause and effect, 200
Change, 122
Character, 325
Charity, 202
Chastening, 58, 114
Children, 282
Christ and the church, 177
Christ and the promises, 264
Christ and the soul, 286
Christ precious, 163
Christ pre-eminent, 1
Christ's 'Come', 184
Christ's death, 173
Christ's poverty, 360
Christ's righteousness, 327
Christ the Head, 77
Christ, union with, 83
Christian and death, 225

Christian, the weak, 229
Church, 91, 177
Commendation, 231
Communion, 98
Companionship, 344
Conceit, 211
Conduct, 251
Confession, 234
Conscience, 39, 239, 289
Consistent, 251
Contraries, 80
Conversion, 276
Covetousness, 244, 300, 311
Critic, 353
Cross, 10
Cure, 45
Custom, 31

Darkest before dawn, 107
Darkness, 307
Death, 132, 147, 173, 225
Deception, 97
Desire, 166
Despair, 154, 266
Despisers, 193
Despondency, 195
Devil, 59, 86, 130, 138, 297, 310
Diligence, 204
Divines, 88

Doubts, 71
Dress, 252
Drunkenness, 78
Duty, 277

Effect, 200
Enemy, 230
Envy, 93
Equality, 304
Error, 13, 244
Esau, 4
Eternity, 7
Evil, 39, 298, 311, 320, 344
Evangelist, 69
Example, 50
Experience, 23
Extremes, 87
Eye, 141

Faith, 36, 106, 253
Faith and assurance, 17
Faith and hope, 52
Faith and other graces, 75, 312
Faith and prayer, 205
Faith and reason, 190
Faith and works, 90, 271, 302
Faith, doubts and unbelief, 71
Faith essential, 131
Faith, little, 261
Faith, precious, 278

INDEX OF SUBJECTS

Faith, temporary, 148
Faith tried, 212
Fall, the, 306, 349
Falsehood, 324
Falsity, 30, 148, 194, 224
Fasting, 125
Fear, 132, 184
Fear of God, 221
Feasting, 125
Final perseverance, 366
Fitness, 128
Flattery, 157
Flesh, 54
Following, 194
Folly, 174, 285
Fools, 174
Forgiveness, 281
Forsaken, 322
Free grace, 206
Freewill, 206
Friendship, 230, 259, 298, 344

Gain, 132
Gifts, 235
Glory, 27, 103, 279
God forsaking men, 322
God, friend or enemy, 230
God, his attributes, 186
God, his being, 156
God, his existence, 255
God, his faithfulness, 198
God, his longsuffering, 332
God, his protection and restraint of us, 65
God, his sovereignty, 176
God, light, love and spirit, 51
God not author of sin, 33
Godliness, 232
Godly, 342
Good and bad, 50, 247, 359
Goodness, 40
Gospel, 42, 213
Governors, 139
Grace and gifts, 235
Grace and glory, 279
Grace and graces, 219
Grace and nature, 73
Grace and sin, 109
Grace free, 206
Grace, power of, 168
Graces, 75, 219
Graves, 143
Great and small, 99
Guilt, 245

Haste, 61
Head, 334
Health, 329
Hearing, 85, 175
Heart, 102, 207, 238, 290, 328,

Heart (cont'd), 334
Heaven, 21, 63, 113, 346, 351
Hell, 113
Heredity, 35
Heresy, 269
Holiness, 273, 329, 348, 351
Home, 339
Honour, 37
Hope, 52, 312, 330
Hospitality, 246
House, 339
House of God, 355
Human frailty, 337, 357
Humility, 30, 145, 361
Husbands, 362
Hypocrisy, 74
Hypocrites, 21, 217, 299, 353

Idleness, 218, 313
Idolatry, 354
If, 155
Ignorance, 209
Ill-nature, 254
Impossibilities, 178
Inconsistency, 291
Influence, 247
Ingratitude, 317
Instruments, God's strange, 6
Inward, 153

Jesting, 92
Joy, 273
Judges, 196
Judging, 270
Judgment, 124
Justice, 34, 55
Justification, 103, 271

Keeping, 238, 365
Knowledge 11, 100, 120, 256, 314, 331

Law of God, 81, 213, 365
Laws, 196
Lawyers, 88
Laziness, 313
Liberality, 111, 280
Liberty, 288
Life, 115, 290
Light, 51, 307
Little things, 119, 261
Longsuffering, 332
Love 51, 267, 312, 336
Loyalty, 240
Luxury, 340

Magistrates, 196
Malice, 104
Marriage, 159
Martyrs, 12

INDEX OF SUBJECTS

Masters, 139
May be, 60
Meanness, 111
Means of grace, 292
Meditation, 319, 363
Meekness, 135
Melancholy, 268
Memory, 352
Men, 99, 185, 322, 359,
Mercies, 5, 16
Mercy, 46, 55, 263
Mind, 49
Ministers, 64
Ministry, 260
Mirth, 92
Miser, 127
Misery, 263
Modesty, 265
Murmuring, 257

Natural man, 73, 275
Negligence, 343
Nemesis, 283
New birth, 281

Obedience, 256, 314, 350
Old age, 241
Omissions, 164
Opportunity, 112
Ordinances, 121

Outward, 153

Paradoxes, 140
Pardon, 82, 146
Parents, 282
Patience, 318
Peace, 187
Pedigree, 35
Persecution, 8, 217
Persecutors, 345
Perseverance, 70, 366
Pharisee, 364
Physicians, 88
Pleasure, 323, 356
Poor, 280
Possibilities, 178
Poverty, 232, 360
Power, 81
Praise, 236, 308
Prayer, 41, 172, 205, 248, 262, 274, 363
Preachers, 64, 79
Preaching, 175
Presumption, 53, 266
Prevention, 45
Pride, 47, 222, 361
Procrastination, 214
Professors, 158
Promises, 226, 248, 264, 274
Prophets, 69

391

Prosperity, 188, 243, 293
Protection, 65
Proud, the, 28
Providence, 149
Punishment, 18

Quietness, 187

Rain, 32
Reading, 192
Reason, 190
Recompense, 97
Regeneration, 208
Relationships, 105
Religion, 294, 333
Repentance, 4, 24, 82, 315
Reproof, 108, 216
Reputation, 134, 325
Responsibility, 89
Restraint, 65, 144
Riches, 227, 284, 320
Righteousness, 327
Rules, 162
Rumour, 171

Sabbath, 191
Saints, 40, 242
Salvation, 284
Sanctification, 103
Scripture, 94, 152, 181, 203

Secrets, 167
Security, 356
Self, 249
Self-examination, 223
Self-righteousness, 327
Sermons, 338
Service, 126, 295
Shame, 245
Sheep, 296
Shirking, 89
Silence, 2
Simplicity, 120
Sin, 33, 142
Sin and death of Christ, 173
Sin and grace, 109
Sin and heaven, 63
Sin and judgment, 124
Sin and Satan, 86
Sin, growth of, 216
Sin, growth in, 179
Sin in the best, 44
Sin its own punishment, 18
Sin of slander, 285
Sin spared and defended, 66
Sincerity, 272
Sinner's verdict, 303
Slander, 95, 285
Society, 117
Solitude, 305
Sonship, 58

INDEX OF SUBJECTS

Soul, 72, 286, 309, 329, 341
Soul-winning, 258
Sovereignty of God, 176
Speech, 180, 321
Spirit, 51, 54, 181, 187, 341
Spiritualities, 210, 220
Strife, 287
Strong drink, 165
Submission, 335
Suicide, 15
Superstition, 38
Swearing, 62
Swine, 296
Sympathy, 67

Talk, 68
Tears, 76
Temperance, 144
Temptation, 25, 161, 218
Thankfulness, 19
Theft, 29
There may be, 60
Things, 119, 150, 167, 210, 220
Thoughts, 199, 250
Time, 237, 301
Times, 316
To-day, 316
Tongue, 358
Transgressors, 228
Treasure, 337

Troubles, 243, 347
Truth, 13, 233

Unbelief, 71, 189
Uncertainty, 227
Uncleanness, 265
Unfaithfulness, 79
Ungodly, 342
Union, 83
Unthankfulness, 151
Unworthiness, 96
Usury, 215

Vacillation, 133
Vanity, 37, 250, 333
Verdict, 303
Vows, 62

War, 160
Warnings, 326, 344
Will for the deed, 9
Willing, 295
Wisdom, 120
Wishes, 137
Wit, 92
Witness, 26
Wives, 362
Women, 185
Words, 137
Work, 169

Works, 90, 271, 302
World, 91, 130, 201, 309, 323, 336
Worldlings, 182
Worship, 56
Writing, 192

Yielding, 25
Youth, 241

Zeal, 14, 100, 224

Notes